A DETAILED HISTORY OF
RAF MANSTON
1931-1940
Arise To Protect

JOE BAMFORD AND JOHN WILLIAMS

FONTHILL

Dedicated To All the Staff at Manston Airport

Fonthill Media Limited
Fonthill Media LLC
www.fonthillmedia.com
office@fonthillmedia.com

First published in the United Kingdom and the United States of America 2015

British Library Cataloguing in Publication Data:
A catalogue record for this book is available from the British Library

ISBN 978-1-78155-095-3

Typeset in 10pt on 13pt Sabon
Printed and bound in Great Britain by
CPI Group (UK) Ltd, Croydon, CR0 4YY

CONTENTS

CONTENTS

Acknowledgements

On Wednesday 15 January 2014, John Williams and I launched *A Detailed History of RAF Manston 1916–1930* at the Holiday Inn Express (previously the Prospect Inn). Perhaps it is appropriate that, at the beginning of our second book, we take a moment to thank those involved with the launch of the first. The launch was a great success, with many friends and local dignitaries present—including the mayors of the local boroughs, Margate and Broadstairs. Thanks must go to Mr Otteson, the general manager, for first suggesting that we hold the launch there, and for providing wine and refreshments. We spent a very pleasant afternoon catching up with old friends and talking to new ones, such as Marcus Russell and Mat from the Manston Spitfire and Hurricane Memorial Building. It felt that we had reconnected the link between the old Prospect Inn and RAF Manston.

There are a number of people to thank for allowing us to use their photographs in the writing of this book—their contributions are invaluable. Firstly, thank you to Mr John Wilson, whose uncle, Aircraftman Fred Wilson, is mentioned in the text. With John lies the credit for providing the photograph used for the front cover of *A Detailed History of RAF Manston 1916–1930*—we failed to do so in that book.

We also thank Geoff Nutkins for permission to use his painting for the cover, which depicts the last flight of Luftwaffe pilot Lieutenant Josef Schauff on 24 July 1940. Also, many thanks to the Margate Museum for allowing us to publish photographs of Ramsgate Airport from its archive, and to Robin Brooks for the photographs and permission to quote from his article on the Pickett Hamilton Fort.

Peter Gallagher has become an integral part of our team and has contributed a lot of valuable material for this book; in recognition of this, his name has been included on the front cover. Peter has never failed to provide for whatever we have asked of him. For instance, he was instrumental in providing information regarding who may have shot down the Dornier which was recovered from the sea by the Royal Air Force Museum in 2013.

There are many other people who have helped and provided both information and inspiration for this book—amongst them Norman Hurst, Derek Crow-Brown, David Stead, Peter Turner, and Wing Commander David Lainchbury. Due to recent events there has been an upsurge in interest in the history of RAF Manston, and it is our hope that this book will keep alive the spirit of those who served at Manston during and after both world wars.

Introduction

The second instalment in a series concerned with the history of RAF Manston, this book covers the period from 1931–1940. The sub-title of this book is 'Arise To Protect', but, as some readers may be aware, RAF Manston was not awarded its badge and crest until November 1948. However, we consider that the motto displayed on its crest was far more appropriate for the period covering 1940—when that is exactly what many courageous pilots did.

Shortly after the first book was published on 19 December 2013, it was announced by the new owner of Manston that there would be a forty-five-day consultation period concerning the possible closure of the airport. Just a few days later that statement was followed up with an announcement that the airport was to close for flying operations on 9 April.

Thanks to local MP Roger Gale that deadline was put back, and between 19 March and the middle of May a lot of things happened—including the Dutch airline KLM ending its twice-daily service between Manston and Amsterdam. Various offers were extended to buy the airport back, but none of them were accepted and on 15 May the airport closed. That was a very sad day—not least because 150 jobs were lost, but also because ninety-eight years of aviation came to an end in such a sudden and unnecessary way.

As this book goes to press, the latest news is that the local authority, Thanet District Council, is going to apply for a Compulsory Purchase Order to obtain control over the airport and turn it into a viable business. There are local people who will take every opportunity to protest against the noise and development of the airport; not only do they have no sense of history or economics, but they have no sense full stop. Manston has a wide, 9,000-feet runway with the capacity to deal with the largest aircraft, such as the A380. It is not logical to build another airport in the Estuary (Boris Island), or a third runway at Heathrow, when such a facility already exists at Manston.

Although this account covers the period of the Battle of Britain, the authors have chosen not to concentrate on that specifically, but rather provide a general overview of the actions at RAF Manston and the units that operated from there. Numerous books have already been written about the famous battle, and we feel that there is nothing more that we can contribute. For reasons of both space and time it has not been possible to mention every operation or action that took place at RAF Manston in 1940. There were so many collective and individual actions that consequently we have chosen to highlight those which we believe to be of the most interest to the reader.

1

Changing Times

On 22 November 1930, a story appeared in the *Isle of Thanet Gazette* concerning a recent incident at sea that had involved Group Captain Pink, the Station Commander at RAF Manston. It was reported that he had recently undergone major surgery for a medical condition, and had subsequently been advised to travel on leave to the Canary Islands for a period of recuperation. Arrangements had been made for the group captain and his wife to embark on the 14,129-ton liner *Highland Hope,* which was operated by the Nelson Line and based in Liverpool. The ship had departed from London on 15 November at 6.41 a.m., on what was only its fifth voyage, with its ultimate destination being Buenos Aires.

During the early hours of Wednesday 19th, the ship hit some rocks off the coast of Portugal and was in immediate danger of sinking. Lifeboats were lowered immediately, but fog and bad sea conditions prevented them being used. All of the 386 passengers, most of whom were still dressed only in their flimsy night clothes, had to be saved by fishing boats and a number of other small vessels. Had it not been for the brave efforts of the local seamen, who knew the coast well, it would have been a terrible tragedy. However, all the passengers were eventually rescued, and most of them were taken to the nearest port at Peniche, on the coast of Portugal and north of Lisbon.

It was truly ironic that, having been sent on leave for the sake of his health, Grp Capt. Pink should embark on a cruise that nearly cost him his life and that of his wife. It was the second serious incident that he had been involved in at sea—in 1913, when he was serving in the navy, he suffered a serious injury whilst serving on a submarine which caused him to have defective eyesight. Both he and his wife were incredibly lucky to escape unscathed from the *Highland Hope,* yet it is not known how seriously the incident affected his already poor health.

In January 1931, Wing Commander Corbett-Wilson handed over command of RAF Manston and took over as Commanding Officer of the School of

Technical Training with the new rank of Group Captain. During this time, it is a confusing picture as to who was actually commanding RAF Manston, but it is thought that Wg Cdr George Horace Paty Padley, who was already commanding the School of Technical Training, had taken over as the CO.

Grp Capt. Pink, who had been at Manston since June 1929, remained as the appointed CO but due to ill health he remained on the non-effective list. Whilst there is a brief mention in some records that Grp Capt. Smyth-Piggiot took over command from Grp Capt. Pink, there is no mention of him at all in the Operation Record Books (ORB) during the years 1929–30.

The Adjutant was Flight Lieutenant G. G. Walker, who replaced Flt Lt Charles Philip Oldfield Bartlett DSC in December 1929 after the latter had been posted to the School of Technical Training. Walker came from a mixed background of army and air force. In 1916 he had been a member of the Scottish Officer Cadet Battalion, but it was noted that when he had been seconded to the Royal Flying Corps (RFC) in that same year, it was from a Lancashire regiment. Two years later, in June 1918, he had been awarded the Military Cross, yet it is not known whether it was for action with the air force or the army. Furthermore, he may have also had connections to the King's Own Scottish Borderers, possibly serving with them and making a very confusing picture.

Wg Cdr Padley, who was already commanding the station, assumed command of the School of Technical Training again during early February 1930. Around this time a number of the workshops at the school were arousing a great deal of interest from several overseas nations. For example, at the beginning of February, an officer from the Siamese forces visited the school for a tour of the aforementioned workshops. Aside from Wg Cdr Padley, a number of postings were made during this time. Flt Lt A. E. Gliddon DSM was posted in from the school to No. 2 Elemental Flying Training School (EFTS) at Digby, and Flt Lt P. E. Owyer MBE was posted out to Headquarters Wessex Bombing Area. Lastly, Grp Capt. Corbett-Wilson was posted to Boscombe Down.

Grp Capt. Hazleton Robson Nicholl, the Deputy Director of Manning at the Air Ministry, visited Manston on 5 March to inspect the workshops of the School of Technical Training and examine the system of training. The following year the group captain was destined to become Station Commander at the Naval Air Station at Calshot, and also had the honour of becoming the first Commodore of the Royal Air Force Yacht Club. A few days later Grp Capt. M. S. Spicer, from HQ Inland Area, visited the school and inspected the Mechanical Transport (MT) vehicles that were used for training.

No. 500 Squadron was formed at Manston on 16 March as a Special Reserve Squadron. Its first CO was Squadron Leader Siegfried Richard Watkins, AFC, who was posted in from the Home Aircraft Depot at Henlow.

Flt Lt Thomas Bain Prickman, who had previously served at No. 45 Squadron, was appointed as the Adjutant. Soon afterwards, No. 500 Squadron was named the 'County of Kent' Squadron, with the motto *Quo Fata Vocent,* which translates as 'whither the fates may call'. It is worth mentioning that although the squadron was formed in March, it did not receive its first aircraft for another three months. The squadron's main hangar was on the site where, many years later, the first permanent control tower was built. At the time of writing this building is still standing, on the western side of the airfield, just off the Margate road.

Flying Officer F. B. Taylor was attached to the station from Wittering for temporary duty as station Adjutant on 18 March, an appointment which suggests that Flt Lt Walker was either on leave or sick. Taylor's arrival was almost certainly the last movement in or out of the station before it was affected by an outbreak of cerebral meningitis.

The condition—the common symptoms of which are headaches, stiffness of the neck, vomiting, and a fever—is caused by the inflammation of the protective membrane that covers the brain. The station was effectively put into quarantine and the training of pupils at the School of Technical Training was temporarily suspended. A programme of outdoor work and games was soon introduced, as it was believed that fresh air and exercise would prevent the disease from spreading. It was recorded on 26 March that the first death had occurred—that of Aircraftman (AC) Curtis, a member of the recently formed No. 500 Squadron.

March 1931 was not a good month for No. 2 Squadron. In addition to the outbreak of cerebral meningitis, two of the unit's Armstrong Whitworth Atlas aircraft were involved in separate incidents, with one being more serious than the other. The single-engine Armstrong-Whitworth Atlas had been designed as a replacement for the Bristol Fighter and had entered service with No. 2 Squadron in December 1929. The Atlas was powered by a 400-hp Jaguar IVC engine and was capable of a speed of 142 mph, with a service ceiling of 16,800-feet.

Reported in the local newspaper as 'A remarkable aeroplane crash', the first accident involved Armstrong Whitworth Atlas J9561, flown by Pilot Officer Windsor on 9 March. Just after 11 a.m., the aeroplane was seen approaching Manston Court Road from the direction of the airfield. It was flying very low. Eye-witnesses perceived that its pilot was in trouble and appeared to be attempting to land in a ploughed field adjacent to the cottages.

As the Atlas approached the cottages, startled onlookers saw it suddenly veer to the right. Then the starboard wing of the aircraft caught the wall of the gable end cottage, approximately 15 feet from the ground. For a moment it seemed that the aeroplane was going to continue past the cottages, but it suddenly flipped over and nose-dived into the ground. Resident Mrs Horton

This Atlas (J9561) from No. 2 Squadron had a close encounter with a washing line. (*John Williams*)

said that she had heard the roar of the engine and then, 'there was a tremendous crash as if the house was falling down'. The aeroplane had come to rest on a hedge that separated the cottage from the airfield, half in and half out of each side, and was totally wrecked.

Mrs Horton ran across the yard, but before she reached the crash site an airman crawled from beneath the wreckage. She called out to see if he was injured and as he answered, telling her that all was well, a second man appeared, who then shouted to the first man to get his straps off—he subsequently unbuckled them and helped his fellow airman out. She later discovered that the first man who had appeared was the passenger, Corporal Miller, and the second the pilot, Plt Off. C. M. Windsor.

The newspaper was quite right in claiming that it had been a remarkable incident: the two airmen and local residents had an extraordinary escape. It is worth noting that Plt Off. Windsor had only recently been awarded a permanent commission with the rank of pilot officer, and had been posted to Manston in December 1930. After such a lucky escape, promotion may have been the last thing on Plt Off. Windsor's mind. However, the incident did not seem to affect his career and in 1938 he appeared in the Air Force List, as a flight lieutenant in the Combined Forces HQ Staff in Palestine and Trans-Jordan.

The second incident on the 27th proved far more serious, involving another Armstrong Whitworth of No. 2 Squadron. The aircraft, serial number J9952, crashed into the sea off the coast near Reculver, killing the two airmen on board: Fg Off. Charles Richard Fildes Wintringham, and AC 1st Class Leonard Alexandra Ellard. It was believed that the aircraft had suffered an engine failure. The Atlas had only recently entered service, however, so it was also suggested that a contributory factor may have been that the pilot was not totally familiar with the controls. This argument was furthered by the fact that Fg Off. Wintringham had only recently been promoted to that rank in January, having been awarded a permanent commission in the RAF in August 1930.

It was not until 14 April that the quarantine restrictions were lifted—just weeks before a high-profile visit by General Gilleaux and five Breguet XIX single-engine biplanes of the Belgian Air Force on 5 May. The general and his officers were met by Grp Capt. Pink (despite being on the non-effective list, he was still active on a personal level). A photograph taken to commemorate the occasion was published in *Flight* magazine, and depicted Grp Capt. Pink reaching up to the cockpit of General Gilleaux's aircraft and shaking hands with him. Strangely enough there is no mention of Grp Capt. Pink being involved in this event in the ORB.

This was General Gilleaux's second visit, having been once before in October 1930. He, along with his airmen and officers, remained guests of the RAF for a week. On the same day as they arrived, and having inspected the workshops at the School of Technical Training, the airmen from Belgium departed for Worthy Down. The general and the five Breguet machines visited a number of other RAF stations before returning to Brussels on the 8th.

The Annual Armament Practice camp was held during April and May at No. 1 Armament Practice Camp at Catfoss. That year No. 2 Squadron attended the camp and faced stiff opposition from the other three army co-operation units (such as No. 4 Squadron Group, which had already been equipped with the more modern Hawker Audax). Despite the strong competition, No. 2 Squadron won the No. 22 Group Air Gunners Cup.

No. 22 Group had first been formed at East Fortune, in Scotland, during July 1918—when it had airship stations at Chathill and Longside under its command. The group had been disbanded in May 1919, to be reformed later in April 1926 from No. 7 Group Inland Area as an Army Co-operation Group with its HQ at South Farnborough. Three Armament Practice Camps had been designated in January 1932—North Coates was No. 2 and Sutton Bridge No. 3.

Airmen from the School of Technical Training took part in the 3rd Annual Route March Open Competition on 7 May. The event involved eighteen teams from the Territorial Army, and the SoTT took first place—another proud achievement for the school.

On 13 May Fg Off. A. J. P. Groom was attached to the school to undertake Adjutant duties, thus taking over from Fg Off. F. B. Taylor. However, he did not remain in the office long, and on the 27th the post was taken over by Flt Lt Oldfield Bartlett. At the end of May, staff officers from HQ Inland Area carried out an annual inspection of the SoTT. Shortly after, during the beginning of June, a civilian from the Air Ministry, Mr H. B. Wynne-Evans OBE, visited the unit to collect technical data. Air Vice-Marshal Amyas Eden Borton, the Air Officer Commanding (AOC) of Inland Area, also carried out his annual inspection on 11 June. It seems that hardly a week went by without the unit or station being inspected.

Known as 'Biffy', the AOC (a former member of the Black Watch and CO of No. 10 and No. 27 Squadron) is credited as being the first person to use the term 'Archie' to describe anti-aircraft fire. While serving with No. 10 Squadron in 1915 he was recommended for the Victoria Cross, but was awarded the Distinguished Service Order instead.

No. 500 Squadron eventually received its aircraft on 4 June. It was equipped with the first of three Vickers Virginia X, which had been introduced into service in 1924 for the role of night-bombing. The Mark X was the final version of the Virginia; it was the first type of aircraft that was built entirely of metal. The frame consisted of duralumin and steel, covered with fabric and wood. Powered by two 580-hp Napier Lion engines and with a top speed of 108 mph, it was capable of carrying a 3,000-lb bomb load. The unit also had two Avro 504s on its strength for training duties. Special Reserve units such as No. 500 Squadron that were equipped with twin-engine aircraft were made up of half regular and half reserve personnel.

On the same day that the aircraft arrived, a special ceremony took place to name one of No. 500 Squadron's Virginias the *Isle of Thanet*. The naming ceremony was attended by the mayors of Margate and Ramsgate, Alderman P. B. Osborne, Alderman H. Terry, Squadron Leader Watkins, and the officers of No. 500 Squadron. It was an elaborate ceremony: the mayors wore their chains and robes, and prior to the service taking place, the nose of the aircraft was covered with a Union Jack. *Isle of Thanet* was Vickers Virginia Mark X, serial number J8240 'A'; it set a precedence for other aircraft to be named after local towns and cities in order to create closer connections with the local communities.

On 12 June 1926 the School of Technical Training was given approval for its own badge, comprised of an open book at the centre of a round badge, with a crown at the top and feathered wings on each side. The badge was approved by the Air Ministry in a letter (A.M. 13682/31//m2) dated 12 June 1931.

On the 15th the engineering officer, Sqn Ldr Ernest John Cuckney DSC, took over command of the School of Technical Training from Wg Cdr Padley, who continued in command of HQ RAF Manston. A few days later, on the 18th, Wg Cdrs F. E. P. Barrington and W. B. Cushion MBE, from the Air Ministry, visited the school in connection to the changes being made to the syllabus regarding driver petrol courses.

Vickers Virginia J7438 *Isle of Sheppey*, of No. 500 Squadron. This photograph was taken while it was in service with 58 Squadron and it was forced to land in fog near Penn, Buckinghamshire. (*John Williams*)

A week later the driver petrol training course was inspected in a visit from Major M. G. E. Walker DSC RA and Captain G. M. Churcher MC RA, both from the Military College of Science, Woolwich. Two days later, on the 2nd, both Wg Cdr Padley and Sqn Ldr Cuckney attended a conference at the Air Ministry in relation to the training of metal riggers. The school was coming under a lot of scrutiny.

On the 22nd, Sqn Ldr Roy Maxwell Drummond was posted from HQ Coastal Command to Manston for administrative duties. In 1925 he had made history when he became the first RAF officer to be seconded to the Dominions on an exchange scheme. His original exchange had been for two years, but in 1927 it was extended for a further two years. Sqn Ldr Drummond was actually an Australian who had been raised in Cottesloe, on the outskirts of Perth, in Western Australia.

On 1 July Grp Capt. Pink was promoted to the rank of Air Commodore. RAF Manston did not have an establishment for an officer who held air rank and consequently he was posted as Chief Air Staff Officer at the headquarters of the Air Defence of Great Britain at RAF Uxbridge. He was still suffering from cancer, and it is unclear how much time he actually spent in that post. There was no immediate replacement at Manston, and a number of officers such as Wg Cdr Padley continued to run the station as Acting Commanding Officer (ACO).

It was always a proud moment when an RAF unit was authorised to display its squadron badge; in July No. 2 Squadron's badge was officially sanctioned. The badge displayed the 'Hereward Knot' on the background of the RAF roundel. There are various interpretations as to what the connection is, but it is claimed that it was taken from the Coat of Arms of Hereward, 'The Wake', and symbolises that the bearer was the 'Guardian of the Army'. A little while later, in September, the squadron was given permission to carry the black triangular emblem that its aircraft had displayed during the First World War.

That July the RAF Swimming Championships were held at Gosport—the station did quite well, but failed to achieve an overall winner. The lengths of some of the events were of a considerable distance, the longest being 1½ miles. AC 2nd Class Barnsley came second in the mile race, and AC 1st Class Cheesman came second in the half-mile event. Cheesman also came second in the 100-yard free-style event. The Ramsgate Challenge Cup, a water polo competition, was held between the 13th and 16th. RAF Manston did very well by defeating two of the local sides. They beat Ramsgate 5–1 and Dover twice, 2–0 and 4–0, to win the competition.

On the 18th, the first Thanet Air Race took place at Manston, after plans to hold the event at the local airfield at Nethercourt were abandoned due to the weather. A piece of land at Nethercourt Farm—situated just outside the boundary of RAF Manston, in the area of Eskdale Avenue near Nethercourt Hill—had been used for flying since the early 1920s, by aviators such as Alan Cobham. It was a 13½-acre site mainly used by aviators taking members of the public up on pleasure flights. The event was widely publicised in the local press, and it was claimed that it would soon rank alongside other rallies and races such as the King's Cup. The contact for entries was a Mr Harold E. White of the Popular Hotel in Harbour Parade.

The event, referred to in some journals as an 'air rally', was organised by Ramsgate Chamber of Commerce and promoted by Thanet Aviation, which had been established by its directors, Messrs Huddlestone, Barnes, Bicknell, and Turner. The company owned the first civil aircraft to be licensed in Thanet, an Avro 504K powered by a 130-hp Clerget Rotary engine. It was registered G-ABJF and had been named *Silverwings*. The aircraft normally operated from Nethercourt.

The main attraction was the Thanet Race. It comprised two circuits around the island, with turning points at Reculver Towers, the North Foreland Lighthouse, and Ramsgate Harbour Lighthouse—a distance of approximately 50 miles. The meeting was opened by Lord Halsbury and the Mayor of Ramsgate, Alderman Terry, with six competitors taking part in the main event: the air race.

Judged by handicap, the winner was Captain Pennington, in a Puss Moth, with an average speed of 128 mph. In second place was Mr Harold Harrington

A.T.S. No. 4. S.F.T.S.
WINNERS OF IRAQ. COMMAND FOOTBALL LEAGUE. 1939-1940.
F/S STEELE   CPL DAVIES   CPL ALBERRY   AC CILL   LAC WOOLLARD   F/O WATSON   LAC FEILDEN
F/LT CLOWES   C/CAPT L F FORBES   F/S FEAR
MC
LAC ATTWOOD   LAC READ   LAC WYLD

The Commanding Officer of No. 500 Squadron between July 1931 and July 1933, Group Captain L. F. Forbes (centre-middle row). This photograph was taken at RAF Habbaniya, in Iraq, while Forbes was serving with No. 4 SFTS. (*Author's collection*)

Balfour MC, the Member of Parliament for Thanet who had been elected in 1929. Having joined the 60th Rifles in 1914, Balfour had transferred to the RFC. He served on Nos 60, 43, and 40 Squadrons before returning to No. 43 Squadron, on which he had his greatest success flying Sopwith Camels.

The Sydney-born General Percival clocked the fastest speed: 135 mph. The prize was a large silver twin-handled trophy, which was named the Vye Cup after the Kentish greengrocers who had sponsored it. It was referred to in some publications as 'The Flying Trophy'. There were displays by a number of aircraft, including one by an Autogiro and another by the Lyon's Tea Company's Falke Sailplane.

No. 502 'Ulster' Squadron flew into Manston for two weeks of training on 20 July. The unit, which was based at Aldergrove Belfast, had been formed in May 1925. It was another Special Reserve unit, and was equipped with the Handley Page Hyderabad, which was powered by two 500-hp Napier Lion engines and had the distinction of being the last wooden heavy bomber to enter service with the RAF. Only forty-four Hyderabads were built. An exercise organised by the Air Defence of Great Britain took place between the 21st and 23rd, and both No. 502 'Ulster' Squadron and RAF Manston played a small part in it.

Renowned Naval Air Service 'Ace' Flt Lt Charles Philip Oldfield Bartlett DSC assumed command of the SoTT at the end of July, while Sqn Ldr Cuckney

Three Virginias of 500 Squadron fly across the airfield, in close formation. (*Kent Newspapers*)

went on leave. Born in Weston-Super-Mare in 1889, Bartlett had joined the Royal Navy Air Service (RNAS) in 1916 and was awarded his Royal Aero Club Certificate in June of that year. He later served with No. 5 Squadron, completed 101 sorties, and was credited with eight victories, for which he was awarded the DSC. Early in August a new syllabus was introduced at the school, and the period of training for driver petrol pupils was extended to five months.

Wg Cdr Leslie Frederick Forbes MC was posted to Manston at the end of July to take over the command of No. 500 Squadron from Sqn Ldr Watkins. Forbes had been promoted from squadron leader at the beginning of 1931, and his name appeared in the *London Gazette* alongside that of Wg Cdr Padley, who had also been promoted to that rank at the same time.

Wg Cdr Forbes was a long-serving officer who had joined the Shropshire Light Infantry before transferring to the RFC. He had served in Iraq and commanded an Armoured Car Company in Palestine. He was previously posted to No. 500 Squadron in Egypt, where he had been the Deputy Commanding Officer (DCO) for No. 4 Flying Training School.

Another distinguished officer, Sqn Ldr Denis Osmond Mulholland AFC, third son of J. H. Mulholland, JP of Donaghadee County Ireland, was posted to Manston at the beginning of September for administrative duties. He had been awarded Royal Aero Club Certificate Number 2111 in November 1915 and had served with No. 40 Squadron during the First World War, when he was credited with destroying at least one enemy aircraft. He later commanded No. 16 Squadron between 1928 and 1931.

There was a visit to Manston in September by two Mexican officials, Assistant Attaché Colonel Castresjon and Captain Don R. Fuenta of the Mexican Flying Corps. The Mexican officers toured the workshops on 12 September and stayed for the night. Sqn Ldr Drummond, who had arrived in June, was posted out to the Army School of Co-operation.

Grp Capt. Sydney William Smith was posted to Manston at the beginning of October, and he took over as the permanent CO from Air Cdre Pink. He had come from No. 204 Squadron—which was equipped with the Short Southampton flying boat and based at Mountbatten—where he had been station commander. He had quite a lot of experience on flying boats; he had begun his military career in 1911 when he joined the 1st Welsh Howitzer Brigade, but re-mustered to the RFC after being awarded his Royal Aero Club Certificate (Number 606) in August 1913. In June 1930, he had led a flight of flying boats from Mountbatten to Iceland and back again.

On 10 October 1931 the airmen of No. 500 Squadron held a dance at the Dreamland complex in Margate, which can trace its origins to 1919—when the light-railway rollercoaster (now Grade II Listed) was opened. During my time at RAF Manston in the late 1960s and early '70s, the delights of Dreamland were still a popular attraction for both servicemen and locals; it is a pity that the site has been so troubled in more recent years.

Also in October, following the naming ceremony of *Isle of Thanet* in June, another of No. 500 Squadron's Virginias was named *City of Canterbury*. The serial number of the aircraft that was to carry the name of the city was J7566, and the ceremony was carried out by the Mayor of Canterbury. The purpose of such events was to encourage the men of the local population to join the unit, and to create closer ties to the RAF Auxiliary Service within the communities of Thanet and Canterbury.

At the beginning of October, AC 2nd Class W. Barnsley, who had done so well at the previous championships in July, won the RAF Swimming Championships for the second year in a row. He won the 100-, 200- and 400-yard competitions, and was subsequently chosen to represent the Combined Services Team.

On the 31st, Wg Cdr Padley resumed command of the School of Technical Training from Sqn Ldr Cuckney. Air Cdre Norman Duckworth MacEwen, the Air Officer Commanding (AOC) of No. 22 Group, was back at Manston at the beginning of November in order to present the Distinguished Flying Medal to Corporal John George Lewis (362477) of No. 2 Squadron. Cpl Lewis was a former apprentice who had trained at RAF Halton during 1922 in the fifth entry, which was the first course held at Halton. Apprentices on the first four entries had trained at RAF Cranwell. Cpl Lewis' award was recorded in the *London Gazette* on 26 June 1931—it had been awarded for his actions while serving on the North-West Frontier in India.

By the last day of December 1931, 453 pupils had passed out of the SoTT that year. The breakdown of the different trades below is an indication of how the RAF was changing—especially in relation to the training of metal riggers and workers, as well as traditional carpenters. It was only in January 1929 that the first course of metal rigging had been introduced on the syllabus for apprentices at Halton.

Carpenters:	38
Blacksmiths & Welders:	38
Carpenter Riggers:	8
Carpenter & Metal Riggers:	44
Driver Petrol:	230
Fabric Workers:	10
Fitters DP:	79
Metal Riggers:	7
Coach Painters:	5

Additionally, the school had trained twenty-nine naval ratings who had been on a Fabric Workers Course, and eight members of the Auxiliary Air Force Special Reserve. Also, a further 136 reservists had undergone their annual training in the trades of carpentry, rigging, and fitting, and 139 non-commissioned officers (NCOs) had undergone courses in metal rigging. The SoTT was a flourishing and busy place that had changed a lot since its foundation in 1920.

2

A Sad Loss

Group Captain Smith retained command of Headquarters RAF Manston at the beginning of 1932. There were eight officers on the strength of the School of Technical Training, with Wing Commander Padley in command and Squadron Leader Cuckney as his deputy. Other officers included Flight Lieutenants C. P. O. Bartlett, G. T. H. Pack, S. Graham, Warne-Browne, and J. H. Pool.

By this time, the lives of the three airmen who had first landed on the Isle of Thanet in 1912, and had influenced the development of RAF Manston, had taken three very different courses. Lieutenant Spenser Grey, who at one point had been Winston Churchill's flying instructor, had retired and was no longer actively flying. Air Commodore Charles Rumney Samson had also retired, but he had died in February 1931—aged only forty-seven. Only Air Vice-Marshal (Lieutenant in 1911) Arthur Murray Longmore was still actively serving; he had held the post of Commandant of the RAF College at Cranwell since 1929.

At the beginning of 1932, RAF Manston and the SoTT were inspected by a number of senior officers, including, on 23 February, Group Captain Charles *Humphrey Kingsman* Edmonds DSO—who was the former Commanding Officer of No. 21 Group (Training) and had just taken up the post of Deputy Director of Manning at the Air Ministry. The following day the school was inspected by Australian-born Air Cdre Peregrine Forbes Morant Fellowes, the Air Officer Commanding of No. 23 Group, who retired from the RAF shortly after.

March was a particularly sad month. On Monday 7 March the former CO of Manston, Air Cdre Richard Charles Montagu Pink, passed away in Princess Mary's RAF Hospital at Halton in Buckinghamshire. Born in Winchester on 30 November 1888, he was the son of architect Charles Richard Pink and his wife Florence Anna. Air Cdre Pink was educated at a school in Eastbourne, and attended the Britannia Naval College at Dartmouth before joining the Royal Navy as a midshipman in 1904. In 1915 he had trained as an airship pilot, and two years later he was given command of two airship stations at Longside in Scotland and Pembroke in Wales.

In August 1919 he had been awarded a permanent commission as a Lieutenant Colonel (Wing Commander), before taking up the post of Director of Flying and Airship Advisor to the Chief of Air Staff. After he had transferred from the staff branch to the flying branch in January 1920, he was removed from the navy list and awarded a permanent commission in the RAF. In 1921 he was been posted overseas to command an aircraft depot in Egypt, but it was his role in India two years later for which he became renowned.

In 1923 Wg Cdr Pink was the Officer Commanding No. 1 Indian Wing, where he remained until 1925. From November 1923, he was also OC to No. 2 Indian Wing, which had been engaged in controlling the activities of dissident Mahsud tribesmen in Waziristan through aerial bombardment and strafing. The campaign, which later became known as 'Pink's War', involved the Bristol Fighters of No. 5 Squadron (renumbered from No. 48 Squadron in 1920), DH9s of No. 27 Squadron (renumbered from No. 99 Squadron in 1920), and DH9's of No. 60 Squadron (renumbered from No. 97 Squadron in 1920).

The main campaign ran from March to May 1925, and resulted in the tribesmen offering the British authorities a peace treaty. It was the first independent action ever carried out by the RAF, who had suffered the loss of only two lives, whereas a previous campaign in 1919 had resulted in over 1,300 casualties. All of the officers and airmen involved in the campaign had been awarded the Indian General Service Medal.

For his part in quelling the insurgency, the then Wg Cdr Pink received an accelerated promotion to the rank of Group Captain. On his return to the home establishment he was posted at the HQ of the Air Defence of Great Britain, Uxbridge. In May 1929 he was posted at Manston, where he first commanded the SoTT before taking over command of the station in July. It is well-known that Grp Capt. Pink and his wife were happy at Manston, and that he was very proud of the station.

On Saturday 14 June 1930 he had held a garden party at Manston, to which 800 guest were invited, including Lord Carson, Sefton Brancker, and Sir Alan Cobham and his wife. Hundreds of well-provisioned tables were laid out in front of the officers' mess and there was a flypast by the Virginias of No. 9 Squadron. The occasion brought together not only the RAF and the wider aviation community but the local community as well.

During his time at Manston, Air Cdre Pink actively involved himself in the founding of a gliding club. With Sqn Ldr Cuckney and Fg Off. Phillips acting as instructors, Air Cdre Pink participated in the club and developed it as the scene of a number of practice flights. One of its members, Fg Off. Mole, went on to claim the British duration and height records.

Unfortunately it was shortly after being posted to Manston that Air Cdre Pink was diagnosed with cancer. Although he was on the RAF's non-effective list for a period of time, he still lived locally and was always happy to welcome visitors to the station. Some time before he died, either while he was still at Manston or after being posted to Uxbridge, Air Cdre Pink requested for his body to be cremated and his ashes scattered on the airfield at Manston.

On Friday 11 March 1932, in accordance with his wishes, a special ceremony was held at the station and his ashes were scattered. A photograph depicting the ceremony shows the lengths that the RAF and the station went to in honouring his memory; his ashes were carried in a hearse along a route through the camp, lined with his fellow officers and airmen. At least three group captains are seen lining the route. A cameraman filming the event is visible in the photograph, on the right hand side, standing on what appears to be a table. Three days later, on the 13th, a memorial service was held in the church on the station; there was a very good turn out on Church Parade.

Between 14 and 31 March 1932 a number of new officers were posted at Manston. The first was Flt Lt F. H. Astle, who took up the post of Station Armament Officer. He was a long-serving officer who had re-mustered from the Cheshire Regiment in 1918, where he had been an assistant gunnery instructor. Flt Lt A. E. West was posted to the accounts office; he had joined the RAF in that branch in 1924, as a pilot officer. The most senior new officer

The parade and ceremony at RAF Manston after scattering the ashes of the former Station Commander, Air Commodore Richard Charles Montagu Pink. (*Kent Newspapers*)

to arrive in March was Sqn Ldr William V. L. Wambeek, a medical officer who had recently returned from overseas after serving for a number of years at Haindi, Liberia. As it might be expected of someone in the medical profession, his appointment was not only mentioned in the *London Gazette* but in also in a supplement of the *British Medical Journal*.

There was further sporting success for Manston at the end of March, when a team from the SoTT won the Tug of War Eliminating Area Competition. Whether they had any further success in the competition or not, each member of the team was awarded a medal.

St George's Day was celebrated in an unusual fashion in 1932. One officer and ten senior non-commissioned officers were detached to Zeebrugge, Belgium, for a commemoration service with the naval attaché. The town had kept close ties with Britain since the First World War; on 23–24 April 1918 a British naval operation had taken place to block German submarines from accessing the Bruges Canal. The St George's Day event was organised with the help of the Dover Municipal Authorities, and a special service took place at a memorial that had been erected to commemorate the operation.

In early April, details of where the twelve auxiliary bomber and cadre squadrons would hold their summer camps for that year were published. RAF Manston had been chosen to accommodate five of them, not counting No. 500 Squadron that was already based there. These included No. 501 Squadron, City of Bristol, No. 502 Squadron, Ulster, No. 603 Squadron, City of Edinburgh, No. 605 Squadron, County of Warwick, and No. 608 Squadron, North Riding. The camps were to be held between April and August, with the first to take place on 16–29 April. The other camps were held at Tangmere, apart from the one involving No. 601 Squadron, City of London, which took place at Lympne.

Air Cdre William Foster MacNee, the AOC of No. 1 Air Defence Group, paid a visit to No. 500 Squadron during its annual camp on the 23rd. The AOC had attended the Royal Military College at Sandhurst in 1909 and served with the Queen's Own (Royal West Kent) Regiment. In 1914 he was seconded to the Admiralty for service in the Kite and Balloon Section, and later served in the Kite and Balloon Section of both the RAF and the Royal Navy; he was a very experienced officer indeed.

In May the station was inspected again by AVM A. E. Borton, who was a seemingly regular visitor to the station. He was to have close connections with the station, in particular No. 500 Squadron, for many years into the future.

The Annual Battle Order Route March was held in May, with teams from the local service units in Thanet competing for the Coleman Challenge Cup. A team from the SoTT won the trophy, but it is not known whether such activities were classed as sport, duty, or torture!

Movements in and out during May included those of Flt Lt C. P. O. Bartlett, who was posted to the non-effective pool at Uxbridge on health grounds, and

Sqn Ldr D. W. Clappen, who was posted in to replace Sqn Ldr Ernest John Cuckney.

Sqn Ldr Cuckney had been in the service since 1915 when he joined the RNAS, and had been awarded Royal Aero Club Certificate No. 2379 on 1 February 1916. Subsequently in 1917 he was awarded the DSC for taking part in a raid on the seaplane station at Zebrugge. Despite the fact that he had served as a distinguished pilot, the squadron leader had up to this point mainly served in staff or administrative roles. However, at the end of May he was posted to the Central Flying School at Wittering for a refresher flying course. He was later posted to No. 70 Squadron, where he was appointed as flight commander.

Cuckney had been at Manston since August 1929 when he was posted as an engineering officer at the School of Technical Training. He would never be posted to Manston again but he had many more years ahead of him in the RAF, and he would rise to the rank of AVM before eventually retiring in 1955.

Replacing Cuckney, Sqn Ldr Donald William Clappen was another example of the rare breed of officer who had risen through the ranks, having served as a private in the London Regiment in 1915. Despite his apparently lowly position, Clappen had managed to learn to fly and was awarded Royal Aero Club Certificate No. 591 in August 1913. He did not transfer to the RFC until October 1915, and in the same month he was promoted to the rank of Flying Officer. Having survived the First World War, in 1920 he attended London University, followed by a course at the Royal Aircraft Establishment. In October 1928 he was awarded a permanent commission with the rank of Flight Lieutenant, thereby consolidating him for a long-term career in the RAF.

There is a note in the ORB that Flt Lt Arthur Hyde Flower had taken over the Adjutant duties from Ft Lt Bartlett, and that he had been awarded Royal Aero Club Certificate No. 4536 in April 1917. Flower would soon be promoted to squadron leader and posted to the record office at Ruislip.

On 6 June 1932 a detachment of fifty airmen from Manston took part in a ceremonial parade in Dover, on the anniversary of the birthday of His Majesty the King. The event was organised by the general officer commanding the 12th Infantry Brigade, based in Dover, and involved two flights of aircraft from No. 2 Squadron performing a flypast. Three days later the station held its annual sports day. At about the same time, Ramsgate held a sports week and many of the personnel from RAF Manston took part. It was a very busy and active time for those involved.

Wg Cdr Richard Cecil Hardstaff replaced Wg Cdr Padley as the Officer Commanding the School of Technical Training in early July. He was another former member of the RNAS who had been awarded his Royal Aero Club

Certificate, No. 880, in August 1914. More recently, serving as a squadron leader in October 1929, Hardstaff had been posted to the aircraft depot in Iraq. As it turned out Wg Cdr Hardstaff later proved to be something of a controversial character.

There were a number of high-powered visitors to Manston in July 1932, amongst them a small number of Japanese officers who visited the SoTT. Lieutenant Commanders Y. Ito and H. Machida and Engineering Officers M. Ishu and S. Morihiro were all from the Japanese Navy. Clearly, the school was becoming increasingly popular with overseas forces.

3

Civil Connections

In 1931 the Thanet Air Race had been held in July. It was postponed in 1932, but on 17 July an air rally was organised and attracted some of the leading names in aviation. One of the visiting aircraft was Puss Moth G-ABKG, belonging to renowned aviator Jim Mollison. Mollison flew there with his fiancée Amy Johnson, and they were married just twelve days later. The Puss Moth was the very same aircraft that Mollison had flown to break the record for the time taken to fly from England to Cape Town, South Africa. In March earlier that year, he had completed the flight in just four days and seventeen hours.

The *East Kent Times* reported on the event in Thanet, and wrote that Mr Mollison spent the greater part of the afternoon in the air and that free flights were offered to those holding programmes. The Sports Avion was flown by Mr L. H. Stace and the Avro by Mr E. Bicknall of Thanet Aviation, while the two Gipsy Moths belonged to the Cinque Ports Flying Club, which was based at Lympne. Other aircraft that took part were an Avro, two Gipsy Moths, a Sports Avion, and a Cierva Autogiro, which was described as a 'weird and wonderful contraption' invented by a Spaniard.

The Autogiro was a revolutionary type of machine; it was a cross between a conventional aircraft and a helicopter, and developed by Spaniard Juan de la Cierva in 1926. The C.8 was the first version of the machine to be built in Britain and like the earlier models, it used a conventional airframe. The C.8 Autogiro was built in association with Avro and used the airframe from an Avro 552. It was powered by an Armstrong Siddley Lynx 180-hp engine, and had free spinning rotors to power it and keep it airborne. The Air Ministry had ordered an Autogiro in 1927. Subsequently a number of different versions and experimental designs were built.

The main event of the afternoon was the 'Gretna Green Wedding', involving a couple who were attempting to fly away to Gretna Green to get married. The plot featured a chase by their disapproving parents who tried to prevent the marriage by pursuing the couple in another aircraft. The final event of the day involved a mock bombing of a car with bags of flour. The car managed to evade the 'bombs' and soon after the clouds opened and torrents of rain prevented any further action. It was reported that the enormous crowd did not feel any disappointment as they had experienced a very full afternoon's entertainment.

The Chief of Air Staff, ACM Sir John Salmond, visited Manston on 19 July to inspect those units that were about to take part in the Air Defence of Great Britain Exercise. It was scheduled to begin the next day and involved the Manston-based No. 2 and No. 500 Squadrons, as well as No. 502 and No. 603 Squadrons which were on detachment to the station.

No. 502 Squadron was another special reserve unit equipped with Virginia Mark X and based at Aldergrove, Belfast. Its CO was Wing Commander R. T. Leather AFC. No. 603 Squadron was a day-bomber unit of the Auxiliary Air Force, equipped with the Westland Wapiti II and based at Turnhouse near Edinburgh, under the command of Squadron Leader J. A. McKelvie AFC. This may not have been the ACM's first visit to Manston, but he was not a regular visitor as were some other senior officers.

On Wednesday 27 July there was a fatal crash involving a Westland Wapiti of No. 501 Squadron (City of Bristol), serial number K1369. The incident, reported in the Canterbury press, happened at Bekesbourne near Canterbury at about 8 p.m. The pilot, Flying Officer Peter Walter Johnson Pharazyn, a twenty-one-year-old New Zealander, was reported to have been returning to Manston from a cross-country flight across Surrey when his aircraft collided with an oak tree. The reality was that he was returning from an airfield near London, where he had attended his sister's wedding, and the cross-country sortie was a cover story to get the flight authorised.

According to eyewitness Peter Ramsay (himself a pilot and a member of the Kent Flying Club), the aircraft dived to the ground in Howlett's Park, slid along the ground for a short distance, and then turned over on its back. During the second impact the aircraft's fuel tanks were ruptured, causing it to burst into flames and fuel a fire so intense that eventually very little of the aircraft remained—except for some metal components, such as the engine.

A passing motorist rushed to help but, in the opinion of Mr Ramsay, the pilot was already dead by the time that the aircraft was engulfed in flames. Fg Off. Pharazyn's body was later removed from the wreckage by the police. Superintendent Goldsmith and PCs Castle, Hood, Chapman, and Scott were praised for their brave efforts in attempting to rescue the pilot. Mechanics from Manston later arrived on the scene to take away what was left of the aircraft, and the unit's CO also visited the scene of the crash. Fg Off. Pharazyn was buried with full military honours in Margate's St John's Cemetery.

The inquest was held in Howlett's Park on Friday 29th; on 5 August some details of it were reported in the *Dover Express*. Fg Off. Pharazyn, who was an undergraduate at Cambridge and was described as a special reserve pilot, had trained to fly with Marshalls at Norwich. His flying record was examined; he had begun flying in March 1930, had flown a total of 360 hours, and had been promoted to the rank of Flying Officer in November 1931. He had flown to Manston from Filton, in Bristol, on the day before the accident to take part in the ADGB exercise with No. 501 Squadron.

It was later revealed, however, that things were not as simple as they had first seemed. When the coroner questioned Mr Ramsay at the inquest, it was confirmed that he was a friend of Fg Off. Pharazyn, who had visited his home on several occasions. The oak tree that the aircraft had collided with was 90 feet high. The fact that the impact had taken place just 20 feet below the top indicated that the pilot was flying very low, and had possibly been 'buzzing' Mr Ramsay's house. Fg Off. George Washington from No. 501 Squadron, who said he had known Fg Off. Pharazyn for two years, confirmed that regulations stated that pilots should not fly below 2,000 feet.

Fg Off. Washington went on to say that he thought the aircraft must have hit a downdraught, and that the pilot had not knowingly breached regulations by flying low deliberately. The coroner pointed out the dangers of low flying and stated that—although there was clear evidence that the pilot was attempting to attract the attention of his friends in the house—he was convinced that the incident was an accident. He went on to pass a verdict of accidental death.

It was bad enough that Fg Off. Pharazyn had been killed on the day that his sister was married, but tragically a few years later the family suffered more bad luck when his older brother was also killed in an air accident on 29 June 1938. Flt Lt William Forster Pharazyn was flying a Gloster Gladiator of No. 72 Squadron when his aircraft collided with another Gladiator. The unit was based at Church Fenton, and the collision occurred over Breighton, near Selby, at 9.a.m. He was thirty-five years old and a very experienced pilot, with 703 hours' experience on type.

Over the weekend of Sunday 31 July and 1 August 1932, Sir Alan Cobham visited Thanet to give an exhibition of his flying skills at Nethercourt. Thousands of people were entertained throughout the afternoon by what he called a National Aviation Display. Captain S. D. Barnard's *Spider* and the Autogiro were the central attractions of the flying display organised by Thanet Aviation Ltd.

Spider was a Fokker VIIIA Monoplane, G-EBTS, which could carry eleven passengers. In 1929 it had flown from England to India in three and a half days. Thanet Aviation Ltd had arranged a full programme of flying, including parachute descents and aerobatic displays by Mr L. H. Stace of Henleys Avian Ltd. One daring stunt involved a pilot clinging on to the undercarriage of an aircraft by a leg and a hand while it performed loops.

On 11 August there was another accident at Manston, but this time on the ground. A Westland Wapiti of No. 608 Squadron ran into an Avro Tutor belonging to No. 3 Flight Training School. There were no injuries, and the only damage was to the pride of the No. 608 Squadron's pilot.

On the 26th, forty-three-year-old veteran of the First World War and 'Ace' pilot Flt Lt Charles Philip Oldfield Bartlett DSC retired from the RAF at Manston with the rank of Squadron Leader. Having joined the RNAS in 1916 as a flight sub-lieutenant, he had mainly served on No. 5 Squadron and flown D.H. 4s. Between July 1917 and March 1918 he had brought down or destroyed eight enemy aircraft. The citation for his DSC simply read, 'For Excellent Good work on the occasion of a bombing raid on Houtave aerodrome on 25th July 1917'. On 17 May 1918 he received a bar to his DSC for further good work, and finished the war as a temporary flight lieutenant.

After the war Bartlett was plagued by ill health. He gave up his commission in 1919, which meant he was reduced to half-pay, but in February 1922 was restored to full pay with the rank of Major. In December of the same year he had been invalided out of the RAF again, but just days later in January 1923 his discharge on the grounds of ill health was cancelled. In September 1926 he took over the Adjutant duties at Station HQ, RAF Manston, before moving on to the SoTT, where he took up the same post in December 1929. The squadron leader had served with distinction in both the Royal Navy and the Royal Air Force, as well as Honourable Service at RAF Manston. Despite the health problems that he suffered for much of his time in the service, Sqn Ldr Bartlett lived until March 1986, when he died aged ninety-seven.

The Right Honourable Sir Philip Sassoon, the Under Secretary of State for Air and Honorary Commanding Officer of No. 601 Squadron (City of London), visited Manston in early September 1932 to inspect all of the major units. In September 1928 he had made the first general inspection of British Air Stations Overseas. He had flown around the overseas bases in a Blackburn Iris II seaplane, accompanied by Sir Arthur Longmore, one of the first airmen to land on the Isle of Thanet. Sassoon was a pilot in his own right and owned a Percival Gull, registration G-ACGR, which he had fitted out with luxurious red leather seats.

After having been postponed in July, the Thanet Air Race was held at Manston on Saturday 17 September with the Right Honourable Sir Philip Sassoon in attendance again to present the trophies. Unfortunately, bad weather and a sea fog prevented the rally from going ahead as planned, although eight aircraft had arrived at Manston throughout the morning. The pilots and their passengers were treated to lunch in the officers' mess by the station's CO, Grp Capt. Sydney Smith. Afterwards, six of them flew the short distance over to Nethercourt in preparation for the race to begin.

A number of officers from RAF Manston were actively involved in the organisation of the race, but seeing that it was not a duty, they were dressed in their civilian clothing with soft caps or hats. Wg Cdr Forbes was the clerk of the course and Sqn Ldrs Mullholland and Toomer acted as judges.

The weather deteriorated throughout the afternoon, and by 4 p.m. it was announced that the race would have to be postponed until the following day. Sir Philip Sassoon was unable to stay over until the Sunday due to prior arrangements, and so could not present the trophies. Also, a planned programme of formation flying by the Virginias of No. 500 Squadron had to be cancelled because of the low cloud and fog.

The following day broke bright and sunny. After further hospitality in the officers' mess courtesy of Grp Capt. Smith and his officers, the competitors moved over to Nethercourt. There it fell to Lt-Col. Louis Arbon Strange to begin the race in his three-seat Spartan Mk. II, G-ABTR, accompanied by a young woman who was described as a 'youthful passenger'.

Lt-Col. Strange was another experienced aviator; he had been awarded Royal Aero Club Certificate No. 575 in August 1913, having learnt to fly at Ewen Flying School at Hendon. He had previously served with the Dorset Yeomanry, but almost immediately applied to join the Royal Flying Corps. In April 1914 it was noted in *Flight Magazine* that he had become a member of the 'upside down club', as one of only five airmen to have achieved the feat of performing a loop. Years later, in 1940, the then Sqn Ldr L. A. Strange would be influential in setting up the Parachute Training School at Ringway Airport.

The course had been slightly altered from the previous year's race. From Nethercourt the aircraft had to fly around the North Foreland Lighthouse, then on to Reculver, before passing over the vaneless mill at Sarre, and then over the petrol filling point on the airfield. Pilots were to fly around the course three times, which had an overall distance of approximately 72 miles. The overall winner, with an average speed of 96 mph, was Lt-Col. L. A. Strange MC DFC in his Spartan. Second was Mr E. W. Percival in a Gull (Hermes IV), with an average speed of 139 mph, who also received a trophy awarded by Mr Bawns for the best performance. Mr L. G. Sparrow, in a D.H. 60 Gipsy Moth, came in at third with an average speed of 101 mph.

Mrs Fairlie and Mr Kirche were fourth in their German-built Klemm (Cirrus III), and had an average speed of 95 mph. The Klemm was designed by Doctor Hans Klemm, who had set up his aircraft-manufacturing business during 1926 in the German town of Boblingen. There is no mention of what type of Klemm was entered in the race but it was almost certainly the Kl 35 model, described as a sports plane that had first flown in 1925.

In fifth place came Mr Windsor in his Gipsy Moth, with an average speed of 103 mph, and there was one aircraft that for technical reasons failed to complete the course. That was a Mr Styran in a Swift (Cirrus III). He retired from the race when his engine began to lose power, and flew deliberately wide of the circuit to avoid getting in the way of the other competitors. As can be gathered from the varying average speeds, both Mr Rowarth and Capt. Dancy, the two men who were responsible for handicapping, had a difficult job in working out the times, speeds, and places.

Grp Capt. Smith called upon the Mayor of Ramsgate, Alderman C. Nixon, JP, to present the prizes, including the Vye Cup, a small replica of the cup, and a number of cheques. The first cash prize was a cheque for £50 presented by Messr Vye and Sons. There was also a £25 cash prize for second place, and £10 for third place. When presenting the Vye Cup, the mayor said that he was sorry that Sir Philip Sassoon had not been able to stay to present the trophies, but he was honoured to be carrying it out.

The mayor then went on to use the occasion for his own platform, announcing he felt that sooner or later Ramsgate should have its own municipal airport, and he would do all in his power to ensure that it came about. In his council election address in 1932, the mayor had stated that he was strongly in favour of a civil aerodrome for Thanet. It was an issue that he had first raised in 1926, but not all the local authorities were as keen as Ramsgate to have a municipal airport.

There were a number of officers posted in during September. Flt Lt C. F. C. Coaker took over as engineering officer, and Flt Lt C. J. G. Nicolls was posted in for medical duties. The Reverend M. H. Edwards OBE took over as the station's chaplain from the Reverend J. H. P. Still. Miss K. C. Watt, the matron-in-chief, visited the station soon after Flt Lt Nicolls' arrival.

No. 500 Squadron underwent further expansion in October: its establishment was raised from three Vickers Virginias to six, with another two aircraft held in reserve. A few weeks later a paid weekend camp was held at RAF Manston, involving No. 5 Special Reserve officers and No. 54 Reserve airmen. Its aim was to encourage local men to get involved and join the RAF Reserve.

On 13 November a detachment of thirty airmen from Manston took part in the Mayor of Ramsgate's Sunday Procession and a church parade at St George's church. On the same day, and almost certainly connected to the mayor's parade, a memorial table in the station's church was dedicated to the memory of Air Commodore R. C. M. Pink. The service was held and the table dedicated by Revd M. H. Edwards—it would have been one of his first major events since his arrival. From what we have seen in the records this was the final tribute to Air Cdre Pink at Manston, an officer who had been widely respected by all those in the service.

There were two more inspections in November: the first by Sir Edward Ellington, the Air Member for Personnel, who inspected all of the station's units, and the second by Air Cdre William Foster MacNeece Foster, the Air Officer Commanding of No. 1 Air Defence Group, who inspected No. 500 Squadron. Air Cdre MacNeece Foster (originally Foster MacNeece until he changed his surname by Royal Licence in 1927) specialised in balloon work.

The final few entries in Manston's record book for 1932 relate to sporting activities – particularly fencing, boxing, and athletics. It was noted that a greater interest had been taken in fencing during the year, which had resulted in two wins for the station team over Wye College. Manston's successful boxing team had become more experienced, meeting and defeating many other more experienced competitors from joint service teams. The station athletics team had also done well, having gained fifth place in the RAF Athletic Championships at Uxbridge. The tug of war team reached the finals at Olympia, but were then beaten by RAF Andover.

At the beginning of 1933 No. 500 Squadron was expanded further. Its establishment was raised to eleven regular officers and seven special reserve officers, and seventy-seven regular airmen and fifty-two reserve airmen. The number of Virginias on squadron strength remained at six, with the two Avro 504N used for training purposes.

Sqn Ldr Philip Fletcher Fullard DSO MC was posted to Manston on 7 January to take over command of No. 2 Squadron from Sqn Ldr S. F. Toomer DFC. He became the seventeenth CO since the unit had been founded in May 1912. Born in Hatfield, Sqn Ldr Fullard had led an interesting life—before joining the services he had played centre-half for Norwich Football Club reserve team. In his later life he was to have close connections with the local communities around Thanet—especially Broadstairs, where he later lived for many years.

Two aces from the First World War and the Second World War at RAF Manston. Air Commodore Philip Fletcher Fullard (left) meets Wing Commander Bob Stanford Tuck. Station Commander Wing Commander Wills in the middle. (*Nigel Wills*)

Fullard had attended the Inns of Court College in 1915 and soon afterwards joined the Royal Fusiliers, before transferring to the Royal Flying Corps in 1916. He learned to fly on No. 24 Reserve Squadron and gained his wings at the Central Flying School (CFS). After qualifying for his wings he became an instructor at the CFS, where he remained until May 1917 when he was posted to No. 1 Squadron, which was equipped with the Nieuport Scout. What he achieved in a relatively short time has been overlooked. Although he had been credited with forty victories, he lived in the shadow of other great pilots such as McCudden and Ball. Also, rather ironically, it was not enemy action that prevented him from building up his score even more, but the fact that he was badly injured while playing football.

January witnessed another tragedy concerning a former member of RAF Manston's personnel; on Tuesday 31st Sqn Ldr Robert Bell was killed in a road accident in Cliftonville. Eyewitnesses reported seeing him driving his car along the tram lines at a speed of approximately 20 mph. He appeared to have seen the tram, which was stationary at the time, and responded by trying to brake, but the brake was faulty and he ran straight into it.

Dr H. W. Parrot, the first medical expert on the scene, stated that the driver was still upright in his seat but was already dead by the time he arrived. The squadron leader had distinguished himself with his research in the medical field, and his death was a great loss to the station. Sqn Ldr Robert E. Bell was buried in Margate Cemetery on 4 February with full military honours.

Sir Philip Sassoon visited Manston again in March, on what the records suggest was a formal visit. At around the same time as his visit, the County of Kent Inter Services Boxing Championships were held at the Winter Gardens in Margate. It was a three-way battle between the army, the navy, and the air force. In the end the honours were shared, with nine points each.

An entry into the ORB on 8 April stated that 'A regular air service between London and Thanet has been inaugurated. A piece of land adjacent to the aerodrome is used as a landing ground for civilian aircraft.' The date of the first flight from the original service from Nethercourt cannot be confirmed, but it almost certainly took place between the end of 1932 and the beginning of 1933.

Edward Hillman had become unhappy with the arrangement due to the unsuitability of the ground at Nethercourt. In co-operation with Thanet Aviation he negotiated an agreement to lease a piece of land at Cheeseman's Farm, adjacent to the airfield at RAF Manston. The lease of the plot was for one year only. The agreement was set up between Thanet Aviation of 3 Chapel Place, Ramsgate, and Hillman Airways of London Road in the County of Essex. It was signed on 30 March.

The ground at Cheeseman's Farm had been licensed as an aerodrome by the Air Ministry. The rent for its use was £160 per annum, with the first payment of

£40 having been made on the signing of the agreement and another £40 due on the first day of June. The balance of £80 was to be made on the 15 September. The rent assured Hillman Airways the use of Nethercourt Aerodrome without any further charges, and Thanet Aviation acted as booking agents for Hillman Airway. For the joy flights operating from Cheeseman's Farm the booking agents charged a commission of 15 per cent, and 25 per cent for those flights taking-off from Nethercourt.

Pathé News filmed the occasion of the first service from the Cheeseman's Farm site. While the exact date is not known, the film was released for public viewing on 3 January 1933. There is also a well-distributed photograph of Edward Hillman shaking hands with Councillor Frederick Pettiman, the Mayor of Margate, and the CO of No. 500 Squadron, Wg Cdr Forbes MC. The flight to Romford took twenty-three minutes, and was operated by a de Havilland Dragon, G-ACAN, which had been christened by none other than Mrs J. L. Mollison (Amy Johnson) at Maylands on 20 December 1932. The service was very popular for a while, and it was estimated that during the summer of 1933 2,350 passengers made the journey between London and Thanet.

During the same period there was a lot of debate between the local boroughs about the development of a municipal airport, and a joint committee

From the Ramsgate pageant of 1934. Councillor A. B. C. Kemp is dressed as the Anglo-Saxon warrior Hengist, with Mayor Alderman E. E. Dye on the right. This was a re-enactment to the ceremony that had taken place in June 1931, when Vickers Virginia J8240 of No. 500 Squadron was renamed the *Isle of Thanet*.

was established to represent Broadstairs, Margate, and Ramsgate. A site at Rumsfield (near Ramsgate) had been chosen by a number of aviation experts, and it also satisfied the requirements of the Air Ministry. Local politics played its part and Broadstairs was the first to resign from the committee; it was soon followed by Margate.

The *Isle of Thanet Gazette* reported events with the headline, 'Thanet's Civil Aerodrome: A Broadstairs Bombshell. Proposals Rejected By Council Committee'. Cllrs B. J. Pearson (Chairman), W. V. Holden, T. A. Pemble, J P, Minter, and Oak-Rind had previously been in favour of the airport project. This notwithstanding, at a meeting of the general purposes committee only councillors Pearson and Minter supported it. There was some speculation that Broadstairs might change its mind, but Ramsgate was left to go it alone. There were still a number of problems to overcome with the project, including various other objections and a battle with the Ministry of Health.

On 5 May both the station and the SoTT were inspected by the AOC of the Inland Area, Air Vice-Marshal Arthur Murray Longmore. AVM Longmore had become the first airman to take-off from land and land on water in November 1911, after developing floatation bags with the aid of the Short Brothers. In April 1912 he had also become one of the first airmen to visit Thanet, when he had made a forced landing in Quex Park. Since those distant days the Australian had been removed from the navy list and awarded a permanent commission in the RAF. He had rapidly risen through the ranks, and in February 1933 he had taken up the post at the Inland Area after serving as the Commandant of the RAF College. The AOC was also involved in training the 'Father of the R.A.F.', Major Hugh Trenchard, to fly. Despite the fact that he had the longest-standing connection with the Isle of Thanet, it seems that he visited Manston on very few occasions.

No. 500 Squadron departed for its annual summer camp at Tangmere during the first week in May. Tangmere proved to be a very popular station with the auxiliary members of the unit and the camp was scheduled to last until the 20 May. The unit played the part of a supposed enemy bombing unit, and took part in a number of valuable exercises.

There was a fatal accident on Thursday 18 May. A Gypsy Moth of No. 2 Squadron, Practice Flight K1225, had been returning from a cross-country flight to Sutton Bridge when it crashed on the airfield, just 100 yards from the Ramsgate to Canterbury Road. The aircraft was one of the thirty Gypsy Moths that had been delivered to the RAF between April and May 1930.

The pilot was Fg Off. Lionel Arthur Hutchings from Watford, who had been awarded a permanent commission on 8 March 1929 and completed his flying training at No. 1 Flying School in June 1931. He had been one of only two pupils to be awarded a special assessment, and at Manston he had been appointed as the Officer Commanding the Practice Flight. A few days after the accident, Fg Off. Alan Harold Hole was posted to Manston to replace Fg Off. Hutchings. Hole had previously served with No. 14 Squadron in Palestine, which had then been equipped with the Fairey IIIF.

In June, the Vickers Virginias of No. 500 Squadron flew in formation over the airfield at West Malling for the opening ceremony as it was about to be renamed Maidstone Airport. The airfield, situated one-and-a-half miles from the village from which it had taken its name, had been opened in 1917 and used as landing ground. From 1930 it had been regularly used by well-known aviators such as Alan Cobham and Amy Johnson, who put on air shows and carried out displays there.

In the same month, two of No. 500 Squadron's Virginias were transferred to No. 502 Squadron 'Ulster' to bring that unit's strength up to six aircraft. During what was a very busy period at Manston, Wg Cdr Robert 'Jock' Halley replaced Wg Cdr Forbes as the CO of No. 500 Squadron. On the 9th, Flight Commander Sqn Ldr Thompson took three aircraft, with six regular officers and six air gunners, to Catfoss for the annual practice camp. Many tactics were learned there that proved useful a short while after the unit returned to Manston.

No. 500's sister squadron, No. 501 'City of Bristol' Squadron, was attached to Manston from its base at Filton on 18 June to take part in the Annual Air Defence Exercise of the Air Defence of Great Britain Command. The Special Reserve unit had been formed in June 1929 for the role of day bomber, and in January 1933 it had been re-equipped with the Westland Wallace to replace the Westland Wapiti. On the same day as No. 501 Squadron arrived, a flight of Virginias from No. 10 'Bomber' Squadron was attached to Manston from Boscombe Down. Also on the same day, a number of territorial anti-aircraft searchlight units were attached to take part in annual summer camps that lasted a fortnight. The camp for the territorial units continued until the middle of August.

Manston was indeed a very busy place during the summer of 1933, with a total of nine units arriving at the station to take part in the air defence exercises. No. 501 Squadron remained at Manston until the beginning of July, when it departed for Biggin Hill, to act as its base during the exercises. The flight from No. 10 Squadron remained until the 9th. On the same day that it departed, No. 502 'Ulster' Squadron flew in on an attachment from Aldergrove, near Belfast. It was commanded by Wg Cdr L. T. N. Goulding MC; it had been formed as a heavy-bomber unit in May 1925, and was equipped with the Vickers Virginia X.

Some familiar faces would have appeared at Manston on the 10th, when a flight from No. 9 Squadron returned to Manston to take part in the exercises. The unit was still equipped with the Vickers Virginia X that it had been equipped with for the six-and-a-half years it had been based at Manston, before it had moved to Boscombe Down.

A flight of Westland Wapitis of No. 501 Squadron, on a detachment to RAF Manston. (*Manston History Museum*)

An aerial view of the camp and airfield in 1933, showing the Armstrong Whitworth Atlas aircraft of No. 2 Squadron. (*Manston History Museum*)

The main part of the annual ADGB exercise began at 6 p.m. on the 17th and lasted until the 21st, with the aim of affording practice to the staff and squadrons that belonged to the Fighting Area and Wessex Bombing Area. For the sake of the exercise the forces were split into two different forces. 'Northland' was made up of fourteen different units comprised of fighters (with the exception of No. 501 Squadron, which carried out a reconnaissance role). 'Southland' force played the role of the aggressor, and contained upwards of sixteen units of both day and night bombers.

No. 603 Squadron, City of Edinburgh, arrived at Manston on the 16th. This overlapped with the attachment of No. 502 Squadron, which stayed until the 22nd. No. 603 Squadron was another auxiliary unit to take part in the annual air defence exercises. Formed in October 1925 at Turnhouse, Edinburgh, it was assigned as a day-bomber unit of the Auxiliary Air Force. On its formation the squadron had been equipped with the D.H. 9A, but in 1930 it had been re-equipped with the Westland Wapiti IIA.

No. 603 Squadron was commanded by Sqn Ldr Hylton Ralph Murray-Phillipson, who was the Conservative Member of Parliament for Twickenham. The unit was inspected by a number of senior officers, the first one being on the 22nd by Air Cdre William Foster MacNee Foster. A few days later, on 26 July, it was inspected again by the Chief of Air Staff, ACM Sir Edward Ellington.

The Royal Navy returned to Manston in July, when Nos 821 and 822 Fleet Spotter Reconnaissance units arrived on the 20th. They were part of the Fleet Air Arm that had been formed on 1 April 1924 after the HMS *Hermes* had been commissioned into service. HMS *Hermes* became the first purpose-built ship to be used as an aircraft carrier, and No. 821 Squadron was equipped with the Fairey Seal, a three-seat Spotter Reconnaissance naval version of the Fairey Gordon. With its 525-hp Armstrong Siddley engine, the Seal had a maximum speed of 138 mph and was capable of carrying a 500-lb bomb load beneath its wings.

No. 822 Squadron was equipped with the Fairey IIIF, which in itself was the type that had been converted into the Gordon. Both Nos 821 and 822 Squadrons were to be based at Manston on a number of occasions during 1933, as well as No. 820 Squadron, which was also equipped with the Fairey IIIF.

Both No. 605 'County of Warwick' and No. 608 'North Riding' Squadrons were at Manston at about the same time. They were inspected one after the other, with No. 605 being inspected on 7 August by the CAS and again on the 16th by AM Sir Robert Brooke-Popham. The following day No. 605 Squadron was inspected again, along with No. 608 Squadron, by Sir Philip Sassoon.

On 18 August Grp Capt. Edye Rolleston Manning DSO MC arrived at Manston to take over command from Grp Capt. Smith, who was posted out and would soon be promoted to the rank of Air Commodore, taking up the appointment of AOC in the Far East. Manning was an Australian who had been studying medicine at Edinburgh University when the war broke out, and in 1914 he had joined the Lothian and Border Horse Cavalry as a trooper. In 1915 Manning re-mustered to the RFC, and was awarded Royal Aero Club Certificate No. 2253 in October 1916. He was then posted to No. 3 Squadron, which was equipped with the ancient Morane Parasol and Morane BB.

Manning had been wounded during the Battle of the Somme—however, his injuries were not severe enough for him to be permanently taken off flying duties. Later in 1916 he was transferred to No. 11 Squadron, and by 1917 he had become a Flight Commander on the unit. In August 1919 he had been awarded a permanent commission, with the rank of Major. Whilst acting CO of No. 6 Squadron in 1922, he was awarded the DSO for his part in the evacuation of staff from the British residence in Suliemanieh, Kurdistan.

In 1928, he was placed on the half-pay list at his own request so that he could pursue his ambition of challenging the record of flying from England to Australia. Unfortunately, he only got as far as Tunisia before the engine of his Westland Widgeon seized up, and although he eventually got airborne again another crash meant he had to abandon the project. In April 1933, prior to being posted to Manston, he had been appointed as the CO of RAF Hornchurch. His official duties as the CO of Manston began on 1 September.

On 16 September a Virginia of No. 500 Squadron, K2670, crashed at Brooklands aerodrome in Surrey, resulting in the death of one of the crew, Fg Off. L. M. Lew. The exact cause of the crash was never discovered, and it is not known why the aircraft was at Brooklands. That said, the Vickers factory that produced the Virginia was based there and it is possible that the aircraft was being repaired or modified. Fg Off. Lew was buried with full military honours, and both regular and reserve officers provided a guard of honour.

In October the station was inspected by the Matron-in-Chief of the Royal Air Force Princess Mary's Nursing Service, Miss Katherine C. Watts, who had been appointed to that post at the end of November 1930. Miss Watts was on the Scottish Register of Nurses, having trained at the Western Infirmary in Glasgow, and had taken over as Matron-in-Chief from Miss J. M. Cruickshank CBE RRC. The main purpose of her visit was to ensure that the living quarters and accommodation were clean, and that the welfare of the airmen was being adequately taken care of.

A week after Miss Watts' inspection, AVM Arthur Longmore paid another visit in order to inspect No. 2 Squadron. These were not the most exciting times at Manston. In November there was a lecture on Air Force Law, given by Wg Cdr Edward St Clair Harnett OBE.

During late October and early November both No. 820 and No. 821 Fleet Spotter Reconnaissance units of the Fleet Air Arm were attached to Manston, with No. 821 arriving on 29 October and No. 820 on the 10 November. The navy was back in some style, and both units were to remain at the station until the New Year. On 1 December they were inspected by Sir Philip Sassoon.

On the same day, the command of No. 2 Squadron changed when Sqn Ldr J. H. Green took over from Sqn Ldr P. F. Fullard, who had only been with the unit since January. Green had recently returned to the home establishment after two-and-a-half years in Cairo and the Middle East. Sqn Ldr Fullard was posted to the Army Staff College in Quette, in India.

The summary for 1933 in the ORB was mainly concerned with Manston's sporting achievements. It noted that the cricket team had played twenty-eight matches, but had won only eight and drawn seven—losing thirteen. The rugby team had done better, having won twenty, drawn two, and lost eight of their thirty matches. It was suggested in the ORB that the rugby team had been considerably strengthened by the inclusion of a number of officers and men from the Fleet Air Arm.

The station football team had done the best of all for the 1932–33 season, having played twenty-three games: they won twenty, drew two, and lost just once. The team finished the season with 42 points, and won both the Walmer and District Memorial Cup and the Birchington Charity Cup.

During the swimming gala at Cliftonville on 20 July, No. 2 Squadron had won the Inter Station Trophy with 40 points, the School of Technical Training coming second with 23 points. Station HQ was third, with only 19 points, and No. 500 Squadron came in last, with a very lowly 2 points.

4

Rules, Regulations and a Court Martial

At the beginning of 1934 the General Duties Branch at RAF Manston was led by Group Captain Manning as Station Commander, with Squadron Leader D. O. Mulholland AFC in command of administration, and Flight Lieutenant G. G. Walker MC as the Station Adjutant. Sqn Ldr W. M. Wambeek commanded the medical section, Flt Lt F. H. Astle was the armament officer, and the Reverend M. H. Edward OBE was the station's chaplain.

The records for the beginning of 1934 are somewhat sparse. In January there were a few postings in and out of the station, but nothing of any great significance seemed to have happened—or at least little was recorded. Flt Lt C. G. J. Nichols was posted to the central medical establishment, and was replaced by Flt Lt J. F. McGovern from Uxbridge.

At the end of February, however, things were to change. The station was the scene of a general court martial, involving Wing Commander Richard Cecil Hardstaff—the Commanding Officer of the School of Technical Training. At the time of his arrest the wing commander was living in Holmecroft, the traditional home of RAF Manston's CO, which was previously known as Rose Cottage.

Born to John Richard and Ellen Elizabeth in 1894, Wg Cdr Richard Cecil Hardstaff had joined the Royal Naval Air Service as a probationary Flight Sub-Lieutenant in 1914. He was awarded Royal Aero Club Certificate No. 880 on 20 August that year. *The London Gazette* published the news confirming his rank of Flight Sub-Lieutenant on 27 February 1915. It was noted that during the First World War he had operated mainly in the Dover and Dunkirk sectors. He had risen to the rank of Flight Lieutenant by 1923, was promoted to the rank of Squadron Leader in June 1924, and to Wing Commander in January 1932. Before being posted to Manston he had served with No. 84 Squadron at Shaibah, where he had been posted in December 1931.

As Hardstaff had been court martialled he could not continue with his duties as CO of the SoTT, and so he was replaced by Wg Cdr Oliver Campbell Bryson GC MC DFC and bar, who was posted to Manston in March. As a former officer who had joined The Queen's Own Dorset Yeoman Cavalry in 1914, he had re-mustered to the Royal Flying Corps whilst serving in Egypt and was wounded shortly after. Oliver had been awarded Royal Aero Club Certificate No. 4284 on 26 December 1916. Just a few months later he was rewarded for his bravery after dragging a fellow officer from a burning aircraft.

On 15 March 1917 Bryson had been on a training flight at Wye aerodrome, a small airfield on the Canterbury to Ashford road in Kent, when his aircraft side slipped as it approached the ground to land. The aircraft burst into flames, but Bryson managed to drag himself clear of the wreckage and then immediately turned his attention to trying to get his passenger (2nd Lt Hillebrand) out. Despite his own injuries and burns Bryson attempted to save Hillebrand, who was still alive at the time he was pulled from the burning wreckage but died, in hospital, on the 22nd. In January 1918 Wg Cdr Bryson was presented with the George Cross for his brave attempts to rescue his fellow officer.

In 1919 Bryson was posted to Russia, where he commanded a bomber squadron in the fight against the Bolsheviks; his actions earned him the DFC. In August 1919 he was awarded a permanent commission with the rank of Flight Lieutenant, but he spent the years between 1928 and 1931 in India, where he was awarded a bar to his DFC. After returning to the home establishment he was posted to the Central Flying School, where he was put in charge of engines—it was from there that he was posted to Manston.

The court martial of Wg Cdr Hardstaff was a lengthy affair: a verdict was not reached until 5 April, when he was sentenced to be 'Cashiered by General Court Martial'. The verdict was published in *The London Gazette* on Tuesday 17th; it simply stated, 'Wing Commander Richard Cecil Hardstaff is cashiered by sentence of General Court Martial'. The affair was also mentioned in the *Dover Express* on the 20th, accompanied with the headline 'A Naughty Wing Commander'. It was clearly not the type of publicity that the RAF liked, as it had the potential to damage the reputation of the service.

No. 33 'B' Squadron was attached to Manston on 30 April from its base at Bicester. The first unit to be equipped with the Hawker Hart, the squadron remained at Manston until June (although there is no mention of its activities). However, No. 33 Squadron was destined to leave for the Middle East later in the year, and it may have been at Manston to prepare for the move.

At the beginning of May airmen from No. 500 Squadron went on summer camp to Tangmere. Amongst them was twenty-seven-year-old Aircraftman Fred Wilson (600114), who served as a metal rigger and came from Ramsgate. Extracts from the letters he wrote to his fiancée Winifred Rose, back in his home town, suggest that he had a very good time. Although the letters referred to his experiences at Tangmere and not Manston, they explain what was going on at the camp and give an insight to the life of a rigger in the RAF Special Reserve during this period.

A group of airmen from No. 500 Squadron enjoying a bit of fresh air, with Fred Wilson on the left. (*John Wilson*)

Another photo of Aircraftman Fred Wilson (right) of 500 Squadron, by the seaside. (*John Wilson*)

In a letter dated the 3 May 1934, Wilson began by stating, 'I'm having the time of my life here. Boy it's simply great.' He continued, 'All I have to do is to do is to just to crawl about the old girl and inspect wires etc. and report anything out of the ordinary'. The aircraft in question was a Vickers Virginia. He then went on to say:

> I went flying Tuesday. I was in the nose. It wasn't a very nice day. Although it was warm it was misty. We climbed to 3,000 feet and got above the fog. I can tell you, it makes you nervous with those Furies about, because I saw twelve take off before we left and we couldn't see any of them now because the fog was too thick. Once above the fog it was clear and very warm. I had to laugh and so did our pilot … as soon as we showed ourselves in the clear we could see our friends the Furies, like Butterflies. They came dashing towards us, looping rolling and spinning just like a lot of happy puppies. It was a moment I shall never forget, as they whistled past like thunder bolts.

Instructions to Special Reserve Airmen were quite strict, and regulations for No. 500 'County of Kent Bomber' Squadron were laid down in document *500S/118/SR/Air.* Pay and allowance for weekend camps was only admissible if the following conditions were satisfied:

(a) Attendance was from 1330 hours on Saturday until 1700 on Sunday.
(b) Saturday night must be spent in camp, unless, under exceptional circumstances, special permission to sleep out was obtained.
(c) Marriage allowance was only admissible for camps of four days or more.
(d) Special Reserve airmen who were unemployed, and whose insurance card was not being regularly stamped by an employer, had to hand in their national health and insurance cards to the accounts officer. If they were for any reason unable to attend the whole of a camp, it was stipulated that they should attend for at least a short period of the weekend and were to have their complete service kit with them at all times.

In AC Wilson's notebook are the remains of notes on the Vickers Virginia. Dimensions of the top tail plane aircraft and elevator copied as 115.75 sq. yards, with the Boulton and Paul manufactured elevators each being 51 sq. feet. He noted that the two rudders were each 17 sq. feet and that the four ailerons were 83 sq. feet. It might be hard to understand how useful this information was, unless one appreciates the type of work carried out by riggers such as Fred Wilson. In another letter, on 7 May, he said that by then he was actually doing the work of a rigger, and described one of the jobs that he had to do:

> We have a plane that is under 120 hours inspection and I am stripping off the fabric and inspecting the longerons, cross-bracing wires and stays. After

that I shall have to replace the fabric. Of course all my work is inspected by an NCO over me. He doesn't have to check much and we're talking most of the time.

Such knowledge would have clearly required the dimensions of the fabric that he needed in order to complete jobs such as the one he described.

In the same letter, he told Winifred Rose that his routine was to get up at 6 a.m. to be at the parade square by 6.30 a.m., where there was drill until 7.15 a.m., before dismissing for breakfast. A working parade was scheduled at 8.15 a.m., when work began. There was a break at 10 a.m. for tea and a smoke, then more work from 10.30 a.m. until 12 p.m. In the same letter, Fred mentioned that he would be leaving Tangmere on Saturday morning at 8.30 a.m., and hoped to be back at Manston by 12.30 p.m. to be with her by teatime.

Fred Wilson was an avid letter writer. A few days later, on the 9th, he wrote again to Winifred, describing a visit by a Japanese prince.

Yesterday we had a Japanese Prince here and of course we had to be just so, you can bet! He came over to where I was working at lacing. I was in the act of pulling a piece of wire on the end of a cord. He asked me if it was to make lacing easier. I stood up, saluted and said, 'Yes Sir'. I did feel a mug. He said 'I thought so', and vamoosed off, followed by several more queer looking blokes. When his back was turned we all took off our caps and bowed. The chaps did laugh.

In the more recent days of political correctness such behaviour or language would not be tolerated, but Fred Wilson only expressed the kind of universal humour that British servicemen have openly enjoyed over the years. He ended the letter by giving Winifred Rose some good news—Flight Sergeant Briggs had told him that he was being put on crew pay, which meant that he earned another shilling per day. However, he had resisted breaking a promise to her of volunteering to become an air gunner—all riggers and fitters had been approached to train as air gunners, but Wilson kept his word. This meant he lost out on an extra shilling and sixpence per day.

Back at RAF Manston, the station threw its doors open to the public on 24 May, with entrance fees ranging from three pence to one shilling. It was not alone in this venture, as other RAF Stations in Britain and overseas also took part in the event known as Empire Day. This was the first time that such an event had been held, so a full flying programme was organised and members of the public were allowed access to a number of hangars and buildings. They were not allowed to wander around on their own, but were escorted in strictly organised groups accompanied by an RAF officer. Approximately 6,000 visitors attended, and the event raised £146, four shillings, and sixpence for the RAF Benevolent Fund.

The station's annual sports meeting was held on 14 June and involved many of the pursuits that its personnel were involved with, such as swimming, cricket, football, and a tug-of-war competition. Just over a week later, on the 22nd, RAF Manston played host to a number of Japanese officers, who inspected the workshops of the SoTT. Amongst those mentioned in the ORB are Lieutenant Commanders Y. Utena and S. Ochai. It is not known whether or not these were the same Japanese officers whom AC Fred Wilson had mentioned visiting Tangmere in May.

Louis Bleriot's epic 25 June 1909 flight across the English Channel was celebrated on 22 June, with ten Hawker Demons of No. 10 Squadron flying from Manston to Paris. In his day, Bleriot would have never have made it that far. He had flown only from Calais to Dover, where he had made a very heavy landing on a small piece of land called Northfall Meadow, behind Dover Castle, at 5.30 a.m. By 1934 advancements in the design of airframes and engine power made Bleriot's achievement seem almost insignificant, but the fifty-eight-year-old Frenchman was still highly respected as a pioneer of aviation.

On the 5 July, ten of No. 2 Squadron's Atlas aircrafts made the long-distance flight from Manston to Montrose, where the unit had been based many years before in 1913. It was a long flight, but the unit returned to Manston the following day.

On the same day, approximately 120 pupils from King's School in Canterbury visited the station under the Public Schools Liaison Scheme. Kings' School, one of the oldest public schools in the country, can directly trace its history back to 1541, when it was re-founded by Royal Charter— and, indirectly, much longer than that, when it was part of the Canterbury Cathedral. A flying display was organised during the visit, and a number lucky pupils were given flights.

It was a busy month, and during the middle of July a historical pageant was held in one of the oldest parts of Ramsgate—Ellington Park, in St Lawrence. The event was a celebration of the 50th anniversary of Ramsgate receiving its Royal Charter in 1884. Such was the importance of the event that the pageant was initially opened by The Lord Mayor of London, accompanied by fifteen different mayors from the boroughs of Kent. Over the next four days the pageant was opened by different people, including Field Marshal Viscount Allenby, the Archbishop of Canterbury, the Marquess of Reading, and the Warden of The Cinque Ports.

Over 100 airmen and their families took part in the pageant, and on the 19th a guard of honour and the station's band were present under the command of Flt Lt G. G. Walker. The guest of honour was none other than FM Viscount Allenby, who toured a number of institutions in the town. Dressed in his field marshal's uniform, FM Allenby gave a rousing speech at the British Legion in Ramsgate, during which he named the building Allenby House and declared that 'We did not fight for glory. We fought because it was our duty'.

Aiming a prophetic station at the younger members in the audience, the Field Marshal said that the present generation had known nothing of war, but that, 'We fought because we bally well had to, and it is quite possible that the younger generation may have to do the same'. The Viscount, who had been involved in many wars and battles—including the Battle of Jerusalem—did not live to witness the Second World War. He died in May 1936, at the age of seventy-five, whilst on a fishing trip to Patagonia.

There was also a little bit of theatre on the airfield at Manston, for the public's entertainment. Alderman Arthur Bloomfield Courtenay Kemp dressed up as Hengist, an Anglo-Saxon warrior, and met the Mayor of Ramsgate—Alderman E. E. Dye—on the airfield by the side of the Virginia J8240 (A) *The Isle of Thanet*. The scene also included Wg Cdr R. Halley, the CO of No. 500 Squadron. It is thought that the scene was played out for the Jubilee celebrations, and was meant to be a re-enactment of the cereomony that had taken place in June 1931..

On the 26th there was a report of an accident involving an Audax of No. 2 Squadron, at Rottingdean in Sussex. Details of the incident are disappointingly scarce; other than mentioning a fatality involving a warrant officer of the Territorial Army and an Audax, there is no other information. According to official sources No. 2 Squadron was not re-equipped with a Hawker Audax until September, so the aircraft might have been from another unit.

Of those officers who were promoted or posted in and out of Manston during July: medical officer Sqn Ldr W. G. L. Wambeek was promoted to the rank of Wing Commander; stores officer Flt Lt D. A. W. Sugden was posted to Luqa, Malta, and was replaced by Flt Lt C. P. Wingfield (who was posted in from the depot at Uxbridge); and Fg Off. W. H. Gee arrived for duty as an MT Officer, having just been appointed to a permanent commission.

During July and the beginning of August RAF Manston had a number of high-profile visitors. On July 20 the AOC in Chief of the Air Defence of Great Britain, Air Marshal Sir Robert Brooke-Popham KCB CMG DSO AFC, arrived to inspect No. 502 Squadron, which was temporarily attached to the station. On 1 December 1933 Brooke-Popham had also been appointed to another very important role—the Principal Aide-de-Camp to His Majesty the King.

Eleven days after his first inspection, Brooke-Popham was back at Manston again in order to inspect the airmen of Nos 501 and 603 Squadrons, which were also attached to Manston. On 3 August Nos 501 and 603 Squadrons were inspected again, during a visit by ACM Sir Edward Ellington KCB CMG CBE, Chief of the Air Staff. It must have been a difficult job for the airmen and officers of No. 60 Squadron to keep both their kit and aircraft in pristine order, as would have been demanded at the time.

No. 501 Squadron was based at Filton, Bristol, and was equipped with the Wallace I and Wallace Mk II—whereas No. 502 Squadron was based at Aldergrove, Belfast. Both squadrons were equipped with the Virginia X. No. 603 Squadron was based at Turnhouse, Edinburgh, and was equipped with the more-modern Hawker Hart, an aircraft that had entered service in February 1930 in the role of a light day-bomber.

There were one or two units that got little or no mention in the ORB, including No. 503 Squadron (City of Lincoln), who were also attached to Manston from 22–27 July. It had been formed at Waddington, in 1926, as a Special Reserve Unit with the role of night-bombing; it was equipped with the Handley Page Hinaidi. It was not one of the most-renowned reserve units, and there is no mention of it taking part in the A.D.G.B exercises.

Flt Lt J. C. Barraclough was posted in from the depot at Uxbridge on 6 August to take over from Flt Lt G. G. Walker as the station's Adjutant. On the 28th of that month Walker was posted to Uxbridge, in an example of role-reversal. On the very same day, the Reverend M. H. Edwards MBE was promoted to the rank of Group Captain.

In September the wireless telegraphy station was transferred from the former war flight site to the main site, on the western side, where the headquarters and accommodation blocks were situated. It is understood that they were moved to higher ground for better reception. At the time of writing, they remain in the same position. The telegraphic address of RAF Manston was simply 'Aeronautics Manston', and the wireless telegraphy station enabled its personnel to keep in touch with other stations all over the world.

On September 18, the armament officer Flt Lt F. H. Astle was placed on the retired list due to a bad state of health. Astle had re-mustered to the RFC in December 1917, having previously served as a gunnery instructor with the Cheshire Regiment. In July of that year he had been promoted to the temporary rank of Lieutenant. Having held the rank of Flying Officer on his transfer from the army, he had been promoted to the rank of Flight Lieutenant in January 1929, after being posted to No. 4 Flying Training School in the Middle East.

On 20 November RAF Manston was inspected by the AOC of the Inland Area, Henry Le Marchant Brock, who was approaching the end of a long and illustrious career in the RAF. Having joined the Royal Guernsey Channel Islands Light Militia in 1907, he had served with the Royal Warwickshire Regiment before being learning to fly. He had been awarded Royal Aero Club Certificate No. 551 in July 1913, before re-mustering to the RFC and joining No. 5 Squadron.

5

War Clouds on the Horizon

1935 proved to be an eventful year at Manston, but it began peacefully enough with Group Captain Manning serving as the Commanding Officer and Flight Lieutenant J. C. Barraclough as Station Adjutant. There were a number of postings in and out of the station, including Flying Officer L. M. Hooper, who was posted in from the Air Armaments School at Eastchurch to replace Flt Lt J. D. S. Denhome, who in turn was posted out to the same Eastchurch unit.

On February 18 a Virginia of No. 500 Squadron crashed shortly after it had lifted off the ground. Fortunately the quick reaction of the crew saved their lives—but not the aircraft. It is thought that the aircraft concerned, a Virginia (serial number K2325), was being flown by former Royal Artillery Officer Flt Lt F. W. Murison. The aircraft's starboard engine caught fire during take-off and its side slipped to the ground, making a heavy landing, before the whole aircraft burst into flames. There were three airmen on board: the pilot, Flt Lt Murison, Flt Lt Debenett, and Fg Off. Cladder.

In March, Hitler announced that Germany would introduce conscription—thereby breaking the terms of the 1919 Treaty of Versailles, which was imposed after Germany's defeat in 1918. Hitler's proclamation simply confirmed what many of those in government already knew—that Germany's Luftwaffe already had 2,500 aircraft, and that the Wehrmacht had conscripted 300,000 men. Soon that number would reach 500,000. It was clear that such a formidable force only meant one thing; Britain, with its ancient force of fighters and bombers, had some catching up to do.

The School of Technical Training was further expanded in March, when a parachute training course was introduced; the first course began at Manston on the 9th. The length of the course was shorter, but more intense, than those normally taken at the school; however, due to it involving a lot more physical movement of personnel, there was a need for more staff. The school made a request to raise the unit's establishment for an additional flight lieutenant for engineering, and a civilian clerk to deal with the men who arrived for the course's duration of four weeks.

At the beginning of April, Fg Off. Gee was posted from HQ RAF Manston to the SoTT for engine duties. The senior medical officer, Wing Commander Wambeek, was also posted out—to HQ Middle East.

On April 28 there was another accident, this time involving a civil aircraft, with far more serious consequences—resulting in the loss of two lives. The aircraft was a Miles Hawk Major, built by the Miles Aircraft Company under its designer, George Frederick Miles. It was designed to be flown from either the front or rear cockpit. The aircraft was powered by a single de Havilland Gipsy engine, the prototype of which had come second in the 1934 King's Cup Air Race—with an average speed of 147 mph. Registered G-ADCW, it was a variant of the Hawk Major that was designated an M2H. The aircraft was being flown by twenty-three-year-old Mr Arthur Sebag-Montefiore.

Mr Sebag-Montefiore, who resided in Green Street, London, had taken-off from Heston with his passenger, Mr George Manchester Steavenson—a barrister from London, who worked out of offices in Edwardes Square. They had arranged for a taxi to meet them at Manston and drive them to East Cliff Lodge. The lodge was part of the opulent Montfiore estate in Ramsgate, and had been purchased by the family in 1831 for £5,500. Mr Sebag-Montefiore had only recently married Miss Jacqueline Nathan, in 1932, and the couple had a nine-year-old son; Jaqueline was the only daughter of Mr and Mrs L. Nathan of Auckland, New Zealand.

The lodge was set in the grounds of the estate, and had been built in 1794. It would later be occupied by Queen Caroline, who utilised it as her summer residence, before it was sold to Admiral Lord Keith—who employed its proximity to the coast by using it to keep an eye on the fleet in the English Channel. A number of tunnels were built to convey him quickly to the sea. The Duke of Wellington's brother, Marquis Wellesley, later leased the house, and the Duke was also a regular visitor.

They arrived over Manston at approximately 3.45 p.m., and the flight seemed to be going well. Having circled the airfield at approximately 300 feet in preparation for landing, it appeared that Mr Montefiore was in complete control. Eyewitness Fg Off. Francis Guy Mason, of No. 500 Squadron, was standing in front of a hangar when he saw it approaching from the direction of Herne Bay, flying normally. He described the weather as being good, but the sky was slightly overcast and there was strong wind gusting to about 25 mph. Over the airfield the aircraft turned to the right over the hangar, flew downwind to approach the landing ground, and then turned right again. Before completing the turn, however, the aircraft went into a spin and nosedived to the ground, just outside the airfield boundary—some 700 yards from the hangar.

An RAF ambulance was on the scene very quickly, but the nose of the aircraft was buried in the ground and the medics found that Mr Steavenson was already dead. Mr Sebag-Montefiore had been flying the aircraft from the rear cockpit and was still alive, but he was unconscious. He was taken to the RAF sick quarters, where he died an hour or so later.

The cause of the accident is not known. However, it is worth noting that the version of Hawk Major that Mr Sebag-Montefiore was flying, an M2H, was fitted with a trailing-edge flap. If Mr Sebag-Montefiore was unfamiliar with that modification, he would have not have been prepared for what would happen if the flaps were deployed with the aircraft travelling at speed. It is quite possible that the nose may have dropped suddenly, causing Mr Sebag-Montefiore to lose control; and flying at just a few hundred feet, he would have been unable to recover. He had been flying for just eighteen months, and not long before, whilst flying with his brother, he had survived another crash. On that occasion his aircraft had struck a hedge and burst into flames, but both men had escaped with minor burns. Mr Sebag-Montefiore had then purchased the Miles Hawk Major in which he was killed.

Many years after the accident, in 1952, the estate of East Cliff Lodge was sold to Ramsgate Council. The lodge had been badly neglected and was in urgent need of repair, but in 1954 it was pulled down; the estate was later named King George VI Park. It is now a wonderful piece of open land, and is available to the public on the cliffs above the sea. To take a stroll through the park is the most pleasant and direct way to walk from Ramsgate to Broadstairs.

It was all change again in May 1935, when Sqn Ldr George Maxwell Lawson took over as CO of No. 500 Squadron from Wg Cdr Halley MC. Wg Cdr Halley was posted as the senior air-staff officer on the aircraft carrier HMS *Glorious,* which had just had a refit costing £435,000. After working up, the aircraft carrier was destined for service in the Mediterranean Sea, but it is doubtful that the Wing Commander was on board when the ill-fated ship was sunk in June 1941.

Sqn Ldr Lawson was another of the small number of officers who had joined the army as a private, been commissioned, and risen through the ranks. Having joined the 2nd Battalion of the Leicestershire Regiment in 1914, he had been commissioned in August 1915—but by 1917, when he was awarded the Military Cross, he was still only a second lieutenant. The award of his Military Cross was reported in *The London Gazette* on 26 July 1917, the citation being for 'Conspicuous Gallantry and Devotion to Duty'. He had led a wiring party out to the front line, and despite heavy enemy fire he had erected a heavy entanglement of wire. The citation also acknowledged his courage and excellent leadership.

Lawson re-mustered to the RAF in 1918, as an observer, and he did not learn to fly until April 1922, when he trained at No. 5 Flight Training School.

In April 1922, when holding the rank of Flight Lieutenant, he was privileged to be a member of the first course to be held at the staff college at RAF Andover. The fact that he still only held the rank of Squadron Leader some thirteen years later says a lot about promotion in the pre-war RAF, when most only advanced in rank wearing 'Dead Men's Boots'.

A detachment of the station's voluntary band took part in the local celebrations for King George V's Silver Jubilee on 6 May, which were held in Margate and Ramsgate. A number of street parties were organised in the towns. Many years later, in an interview with the *Thanet Gazette*, local resident Rosa Setterfield recalled that some of them went on all night. Rosa reminisced about leaving a dance hall in St Luke's Avenue in the early hours of the morning, and being quite surprised to find people still out singing and dancing. Lyons Tea Company had provided free tea and hats, and everyone enjoyed what was a beautiful day. A special celebratory parade was carried out on the parade ground at Manston, which the public were allowed to watch.

Delegates from the Federation of East Kent's Chamber of Commerce were shown around the station on the 16th. The main places they were allowed access to were No. 2 Squadron's hangar and the workshops of the SoTT.

RAF Manston was opened up to the general public on the 24th for the second Empire Air Day; stations allowed access to a limited number of their buildings and aircraft both at home and abroad. That the number of visitors was considerably less than the previous year was an unfortunate sign of the harsh economic times. It is not known what the entrance fee was in 1935; however, the number of visitors in 1935 was 4,300, down from 6,000 the year before. This meant that the amount of money that the station raised for the Benevolent Fund was just £108, 18 shillings, and 10 pence; celebrations for the King's Silver Jubilee, and a number of other events, may have contributed to the low numbers.

Just a few days prior to Empire Air Day, Ramsay McDonald's Labour government issued a statement in response to Hitler's March announcement regarding conscription and expansion of German forces. The government stated that it intended to triple the size of the RAF over the next two years. It was clear to many people that war clouds were on the horizon; their priorities were changing, and events like Empire Air Day did not have the same significance they had enjoyed even in the previous year.

This notwithstanding, Empire Air Day also saw a celebratory service held in Canterbury Cathedral on June 15. RAF Manston sent a contingent, comprised of twenty airmen and a single senior non-commissioned officer, to take part. The postings in and out during the month of June included Sqn Ldr E. Newall coming from Uxbridge for stores duties, and Sqn Ldr H. E. Tansley being posted to the Air Ministry for administrative duties. Tansley was replaced by Sqn Ldr F. Wright, who was posted in from Uxbridge.

On the civil side, there were further developments on Thursday 20 June 1935, when the Mayor of Ramsgate's wishes came to fruition and the first aircraft landed at Ramsgate Airport (flown by Mr Whitney Straight). The *East Kent Times* reported the event on the 26th with the headline: 'First official landing at Ramsgate's Aerodrome'. The landing was made a few days before the airport's licence was issued by the Air Ministry, on the 30th, and the airport was not officially opened until 1 July.

It is worth noting that a number of other airmen had also laid claims to making the first landing at Rumfields, including Mr Albert Batchelor of Bleak House, Broadstairs, who had regularly flown his Klemm monoplane, G-ACXD, on to the site. In fact, Mr Bachelor had kept at least one of his aircraft in a facility on the site. Also, the land that had been chosen for the airport—once described as no more than a stubble field—had been used as landing ground for a number of years.

The 90-acre airport at Rumsfield, barely 1 mile away from RAF Manston, was much bigger than the one at Nethercourt. The runway was laid out in a north-east to south-westerly direction, with grass runways that were 2,250 feet long. The airport was to be run by Ramsgate Corporation, in conjunction with a company that was controlled by the American-born Whitney Straight—a flamboyant racing-car driver. Mr Straight also had a keen interest in aviation, operating a number of airfields and flying clubs at Exeter, Plymouth, Ipswich, and Haldon (near Teignmouth, in Devon).

Mayor of Ramsgate Alderman E. E. Dye, who had greeted Mr Straight on his arrival, was taken on a flight around Thanet before being flown to Belgium by Neville Stack of Crilly Airways, on the inaugural Hillman Airways service to Ostend. Ostend Airport was unfortunately not ready, and the aircraft had to land at Le Zoute, Knokke, further up the coast. Crilly Airways was founded by entrepreneur Leo Crilly, who operated out of an airfield near Leicester. Mr Stack and representatives of Crilly Airways also attended the dinner to celebrate the opening of the airport.

Within a few weeks of opening, Ramsgate Airport Limited formed as a private limited company, with a capital of £5,000 in £1 shares and Mr Whitney Straight, Mr Richard Seaman, and Mr F. W. Gwathen as directors. Ramsgate Council was forced to borrow £4,865 from the Ministry of Health to finance the project. Facilities were quite basic to begin with, but plans were already in place to build a terminal building, a hangar, and a control tower. The opening of Ramsgate Airport meant that RAF Manston had a neighbour that could act as a satellite airfield during busy periods, or in times of crisis. Ramsgate Airport might have been open and operational, but it was not opened officially for another two years!

In the first few weeks of July, the CO of the Practice Flight, Fg Off. Alan Harold Hole, was transferred to the Reserve. He competed in the 1937

King's Cup Air Race, together with another Manston pilot, Flt Lt H. R. A. Edwards. Fg Off. Hole had 1,250 hours in his log book, and flew a Percival Vega Gull (No. 16) for Mr Lindsay Everard, MP. Another officer posted out from Manston at the same time was Sqn Ldr D. Mulholland, who was posted to No. 2 Armoured Car Section in the Middle East. The two most important postings that occurred in July concerned the command of the station itself, and one of Manston's resident squadrons.

The former affected the command of No. 2 Squadron, when Sqn Ldr Desoer took over the command—or 'Boss', as squadron tradition dictated—from Sqn Ldr J. H. Green. It is not known what happened to Green, but he may have gone to the Air Ministry—which is where he was when the Air Force List for 1939 was compiled.

Sqn Ldr Noel Lloyd Desoer, who had served on No. 2 Squadron many years previously, was posted to Manston from the Air Staff Directorate of Organisation. He had joined the service towards the end of the First World War, being commissioned in April 1917 with the rank of Lieutenant. In August 1919 he had been promoted to Flying Officer, but the following month he was placed on the unemployed list—a sign of the times. In the December of that year he was given a short service commission; however, this was with the rank of flying officer. This entailed him having to give up the rank of Flight Lieutenant to which he had been just promoted.

In May 1920 he was part of the Mesopotamian Wing and awaiting disposal, but he managed to remain in the RAF. The following year he was flying the Westland Wapiti from Mosul with No. 30 Squadron. By July 1921 he was in Turkey with No. 207 Squadron, and at the end of the year he had returned home as part of No. 2 Squadron, at Oranmore, in Galway, Ireland. In February 1923 he was made a Flight Commander on No. 2 Squadron; it was his time on that unit that gave him his first real period of stability. He remained with No. 2 Squadron until November 1926, having been promoted to Squadron Leader in July 1924.

Having served at the Staff Armament and Gunnery School for two years, in October 1928 Sqn Ldr Desoer was again posted overseas to India, and did not return until he was posted to the Air Staff in May 1934. Desoer had certainly done the rounds and returned to serve with No. 2 Squadron the hard way!

On the first day of July 1935 the SoTT underwent another change of title, when Air Ministry Order No. 352/35 renamed it No. 3 School of Technical Training. The school had been separated from HQ RAF Manston at the beginning of July 1929, when it had become an RAF unit in its own right. Up until this point the SoTT at Manston had trained men, whereas the other SoTT, at Halton, trained boys—and there was no distinction between their titles other than the words 'men' and 'boys'.

From July 1935 Halton was named the No. 1 School of Technical Training, but there is something of a mystery about No. 2 School of Technical Training. It was not established until 1938 at RAF Cosford, and it seems odd that the SoTT at Manston was relegated to becoming third.

At the same time that No. 3 SoTT was established at Manston, on 3 July an officer's course in the upkeep and care of parachutes was transferred from Henlow. The authority was AMO No. 304/35, and the parachute training course that had been established in March further secured both the school's and the station's future with the Air Ministry.

On 6 July the Royal Review of the RAF was conducted at both Duxford and Mildenhall for King George VI, during which the Virginias of No. 500 Squadron took part in the fly past to represent RAF Manston. Twenty squadrons took part in the fly past and the airmen of No. 500 Squadron were honoured to be one of them, with its aircraft cruising past the saluting base at a steady 140 mph.

There was another change of command at HQ RAF Manston in July, when Grp Capt. Edye Rolleston Manning decided to retire. The thirty-six-year-old officer had served in a variety of branches and other forces since 1914; in the air force he had been best associated with Nos 3 and 11 Squadrons, which he had commanded. Manning returned to his native Australia after retiring, where he joined the Sydney Stock Exchange. It was not the end of his career in the RAF, however, and he was recalled to the service shortly after war broke out in 1939. Promoted to the rank of Air Commodore, he served in Burma and the Far East, commanding No. 221 Group until May 1945, when he reverted to the retired list again.

Grp Capt. Manning's replacement at Manston was Grp Capt. William Victor Strugnell MC and bar, who took command of the station from 26 July. The Group Captain was familiar with Manston having been the CO of No. 9 Squadron, which had been based at the station until it had moved to Boscombe Down in November 1930. Known to his friends as 'Struggy', Strugnell was born and raised in Southampton, and was another of that rare breed of officer who had risen through the ranks. Having joined the Royal Engineers as a bugler in 1907, at the age of fifteen, he had later transferred to the Hampshire Regiment to become a sapper. In 1912 he re-mustered to the Royal Flying Corps, and became the third non-commissioned officer to be awarded a Royal Aero Club Certificate, No. 253, at Larkhill, on Salisbury Plain, on 24 July 1912. On the certificate his trade is listed as air mechanic.

Strugnell had served in the RFC with both No. 3 and No. 5 Squadrons, but when war was declared he had been sent to France with No. 1 Squadron. He was later commissioned as 2nd lieutenant in June 1915. He then went on to serve with No. 54 Squadron, and claimed his first victory on 5 February 1916, while flying a Morane-Saulnier. The award of his Military Cross was reported in *The London Gazette* in June 1916, and by the end of the war he had been credited with destroying five enemy aircraft and one kite balloon.

By the end of the war Strugnell had been promoted to the rank of Major, and in July 1928, after serving overseas in Iraq and Egypt, he was promoted to Wing Commander and given the command of No. 9 Squadron, which was then based at Manston. Grp Capt. Strugnell was posted to Manston from Hinaida, Iraq, where he had commanded No. 1 Armoured Car Company. He was to command the station through the troubled and very important period leading up to the outbreak of the Second World War.

During the summer a number of different units from the Territorial Army were attached to RAF Manston for their summer camps. The Tyne Electrical Engineers were the first to arrive, on 23 June, and stayed until 7 July. On the day that the Tyne Group departed the Essex Anti-Aircraft Group arrived, and they remained at Manston until the 21st. They were replaced by the 26th Anti-Aircraft Battalion, which was attached to Manston until 4 August. The Kent and Middlesex Group Royal Engineers were attached to Manston from 3 August until the 17th, and the ADF Signals from 11th to the 24th.

The RAF reserve squadrons that were attached to Manston during the summer included No. 502 'Ulster' Squadron from 14 July to the 27th, and No. 607 'Durham' from the 20th to 3 August. No. 501 'Bristol' Squadron was attached from 4 August to the 17th; No. 605 'Warwick' from the 4th to the 8th; and No. 608 from the 10th to the 24th. It is noted in the records that Nos 501, 605, and 608 Squadrons were inspected by Sir Philip Sassoon on 14 August.

In No. 3 SoTT's ORB, it is noted that, at the beginning of October, 'owing to the expansion scheme the strength of trained personnel has reached 1,134'. This was broken down into the trades of mates; aero engineer fitters; metal riggers; parachute maintainers; petrol drivers; fabric workers; and metal workers. In addition, there were officers, airmen reservists, and naval ratings under training to be added to that figure. Clearly Manston was playing an important part in the plan to triple the size of the RAF, in preparation for what lay ahead.

At the beginning of the following month it was noted that the school's establishment had been further increased by Amendment No. 4, and that the number of trainees had risen to 1,836. The total strength of the school, including service and civilian instructors, was approximately 2,000. There is an indication that Wg Cdr Bryson and his staff were struggling to cope.

The school may have been expanding, but HQ RAF Manston was about to lose its long-time resident, army co-operation unit No. 2 Squadron. On 3 November it departed from Manston and moved down the coast to Hawkinge, 2 miles north of Folkestone. Sqn Ldr Desour, who had only recently been appointed, was the eighth officer to command the unit while it had been at

Manston, and he, his officers, and his men were very much missed. The unit had first arrived at Manston in March 1924, but three years later it had been posted out to China where its personnel had suffered badly from the climate and disease. However, by the end of 1927 No. 2 Squadron had returned to Manston under the familiar command of Sqn Ldr Sowrey, who had led the unit since April 1925.

No. 3 SoTT was inspected on 14 November by Air Vice-Marshal Charles Stewart Burnett, AOC of the Inland Area. Burnett had an interesting background, having been born in Minnesota, USA, to Scottish parents. Educated at Bedford School, Burnett had joined the Imperial Yeomanry before transferring to the Highland Light Infantry and being commissioned in 1901. August 1909 was a busy month for Burnett, as he resigned his commission in the Highland Light Infantry and took a civilian job. Five years later, in August 1914, he was back in the service and appointed to a temporary commission in the General Reserve of Officers, with the rank of Lieutenant.

Having been awarded Royal Aero Club Certificate No. 985 in November 1914, Burnett went on to serve with Nos 17, 36, and 12 Squadrons on the Western Front. It was whilst he was on No. 12 Squadron that his strange taste for a glass of milk laced with a dram of whiskey caused something of a logistical problem. There was a severe shortage of fresh milk, and Burnett's refusal to accept condensed milk meant the squadron was forced to buy a cow from a French farmer. It became the only unit on the Western Front to have its very own cow!

In October 1921 Burnett was put on the half-pay list, but he went on to become the Officer Commanding No. 21 Group and later commanded the Central Flying School. AVM Burnett had been appointed the post of AOC Inland Area in January 1935, and the reason for his visit and inspection on 1 December of that year was because the station was being transferred from No. 22 Group to the Inland Area.

Manston had lost No. 2 Squadron to Hawkinge, but on 16 November it was replaced by a unit that would soon be re-equipped with the most modern aircraft in service. No. 48 Squadron, under the command of Sqn Ldr Thomas Audley Langston-Sainsbury, was posted to Manston from Bicester, where it had been reformed after being disbanded in India in April 1920. The unit was initially equipped with the SARO Cloud, an odd-looking, amphibian type of aircraft which was powered by two Armstrong-Siddley engines. First flown in 1930, it had been originally used by the Royal Navy at its Seaplane Training Squadron based at Calshot. The aircraft from 'B' Flight of that unit were allocated to No. 48 Squadron.

On the same day that No. 48 Squadron arrived at Manston, future Prime Minister Winston Churchill made one of his first speeches on BBC Radio about the threat of Nazi Germany, and suggested that the country should prepare itself for war. Churchill posed this question: in the event of the country being attacked or invaded, would the aggressor be content to listen to the impassionate appeals of Lloyd George, or that of that most famous South African General Smuts? Rather than listen, Churchill said, the invader might say, 'You have had your day, and now we want ours,' or, 'Now you are weak, and we are strong!' It was a speech clearly aimed at the increasingly-dangerous Nazi regime. Like General Allenby, Churchill knew that Britain had to re-arm before it was too late.

6

The Manston Spy

On 29 August 1935 Dr Hermann Görtz, a lawyer and self-acclaimed novelist, arrived in Britain with his nineteen-year-old secretary Marianne Emig. After spending a short time living in Mildenhall, in Suffolk (where there was another important RAF airfield), they moved to Kent. Within a short while the German couple made national headlines, putting Margate and RAF Manston on the map.

The couple arrived at Broadstairs on 11 September, when Görtz called in at an auctioneers which advertised that it also acted as an agent for houses that were to let. Görtz enquired after any furnished houses in the area, and he was told about a bungalow in Stanley Road that was called 'Havelock'. It was owned by a Mrs Johnson, who agreed to rent the bungalow out to Görtz for an initial period of 16 September to 26 October. Mrs Johnson's husband had been the entertainment manager for Broadstairs for many years, and she lived in another property close by.

Posing as uncle and niece, Görtz and Emig seemingly lived a normal and peaceful life, with the exception of the attention drawn to them by Görtz's Zandapp motorbike—and the strange clothing they wore when riding it. The other strange thing was that Marianne Emig normally drove the motorcycle, whilst Dr Görtz sat on the pillion seat. Emig was described as an attractive young woman, and she soon struck up a friendship with a young airman, Kenneth Lewis, who was on leave from his base at Lee-on-Solent. They had met on a country lane when Lewis had stopped to make adjustments to his motorbike and, with that in common, Emig had invited him back for tea.

Lewis was subtly grilled for information about RAF airfields and aircraft, and he eventually promised to give Emig photographs and information about certain airfields. The cover story was that Görtz was writing a book about the development of the RAF; Lewis was promised money for the cost of the photographs, and a holiday in Germany—which he sensibly turned down. He sent photos and a few pieces of information to Emig, and was astonished to find that both she and Görtz knew more about the RAF than he did.

On 24 October, just two days before the tenancy agreement expired, Mrs Johnson discovered that Görtz and Emig had gone. However, a few days later she received a telegram from him confirming that they had returned to Germany. It was very brief, simply reading:

TWO DAYS FOR GERMANY BACK SATURDAY TAKE CARE OF MY COMBINATION AND PHOTO.

The word 'GORBY' appeared at the bottom of the telegram, which presumably should have been Görtz, and the word 'care' had been written after the telegram had been printed—in longhand, either by pen or pencil.

Görtz followed up on the telegram with a postcard a few days later, repeating that they would return soon and again asking Mrs Johnson to look after his 'combination'. Görtz was referring to the overalls that he put on when he rode his motorbike, which he had left behind the door of the shed at the back of the bungalow. Mrs Johnson, however, thought that he meant his motorcycle sidecar combination—and when she discovered it was missing, she assumed it had been stolen.

On 26 October Mrs Johnson called the police and the auctioneers to report the suspected theft. They went to the bungalow together to inspect the inventory, and were surprised to find extensive documents and photos which suggested that Görtz had been spying on the RAF. The most important item was said to have been a sketch of the airfield at RAF Manston, but there were also reports of them finding a cipher key. An arrest warrant was issued, and it was effected on 8 November, when Görtz arrived back in England on the Harwich Ferry. Görtz was taken to Broadstairs police station to be interviewed, where he protested his innocence; he argued that the photos and documents had been for a book, which he was trying to get published in order to clear his debts. Emig, on the other hand, escaped capture by staying behind in Germany.

Görtz was formally charged on the 9th, appeared before the Cinque Ports Magistrates in private, and was subsequently remanded in custody. According to the War Office statement, he was charged at the Parish of Broadstairs and St Peters, with offences that had taken place between 18 September and 23 October 1935. He was alleged to have acted in contravention to Section 1B of the Official Secrets Act 1911 (as amended by the Official Secrets Act 1920), to have conspired with another person (not in custody) to commit offences against the Official Secrets Act 1911 and 1920. Under Section 1B, a person was guilty of felony (punishable by three to seven years penal servitude) if, for any purposes prejudicial to the safety or interest of the state, he or she made any sketch, plan, or note which was calculated to be, or might be, or intended to be directly or indirectly useful to the enemy.

It is understood that Görtz was taken to Brixton Prison, before being transported to Margate in a metropolitan police van on the 18th, where he again appeared before the court. Dozens of reporters from the national press had surrounded the town hall, most of them having travelled down from London. They continuously walked around the building in the centre of the market square, looking for a way in, but all the doors were well-guarded. Police protected Görtz from what was described in the *Isle of Thanet Gazette* as a 'merciless battery of cameras' as he jumped out of the police van for the short run into the building.

The proceedings were held in a private room in the town hall, and the bench was made up of the Chairman, Alderman F. T. Fasham, Mr Booth Reeve, Mrs Manston, and Mrs W. Tomlin. In the *Isle of Thanet Gazette* Görtz was described as looking between forty to forty-five years of age, fairly tall, clean shaven, of military appearance, and as speaking English with a foreign accent. The *Gazette* also reported that when Görtz appeared, having climbed the stairs from his police cell, there was a ripple of excitement in the court. He appeared wearing a grey double-breasted suit with a khaki shirt, not looking at all like the British stereotype of the German race.

Görtz was said to have appeared tense, and he was having difficulty following the proceedings in the crowded room, filled with a lot of uniforms. Mr Hedley J. Parham led the prosecuting counsel, as the director of public prosecutions. Amongst those in the court room were the Chief Constable of Kent, Major H. E. Chapman, the chief constable of Margate, Mr W. Palmer and the Commanding Officer of RAF Manston, Group Captain Strugnell. Squadron Leader Stammers, representing the Provost Marshal of the RAF, was also present in court. Görtz was remanded in custody again, until 11 a.m. on Tuesday 26 November.

During the session on the 26th, which was also held in camera (private), Görtz was again detained, and then sent for trial at the Old Bailey. The trial was scheduled to be heard in February. It was the first spy trial in Britain since Lt Norman Baille-Stewart, of the Seaforth Highlanders, had been court martialled for allegedly fraternizing with a German woman in Berlin in 1933. From the start it must have been fairly obvious that it could not be held in a magistrate's court.

On 6 December a story appeared in the *Daily Express* about Marianne Emig, after one of its journalists tracked her down to an address in Hamburg. The reporter was met at the door by Emig's elderly father, who was a retired engine driver, and Ms Emig appears to have been reasonably co-operative during the interview. She told the reporter that Görtz had been born and bred in Prussia, while her family came from Bavaria.

When questioned about her relationship with Görtz, Emig denied that it had been anything other than professional and claimed that she had worked for him as his secretary. Emig claimed that a translational misunderstanding had caused people to think that she was his niece, and once that had happened it was easier to let them go on thinking that. Emig avoided going into detail on the subject of what Görtz had really been doing in England, and knew that although she faced being arrested if she returned, it was unlikely she could be forced to do so.

The role of No. 500 Squadron changed at the beginning of December, when it was designated as a single-engine day-bomber unit, with its Vickers Virginias to be replaced with the Hawker Hart. Senior officers instigated the change following doubts that airmen in an auxiliary unit could cope with the increasing complexity of the new breed of heavy-bombers, such as the Whitley and the Wellington.

Life had to go on as normal, despite the prospect of potential enemy spies lurking around the airfield; however, it was clear that the increased activity at Manston had attracted some unwanted attention. At the end of 1935 the results of pupils who had been trained at No. 3 SoTT were given in a table format. This was the first time that the numbers of those who had passed their examinations were given, instead of just the number of pupils who had passed through the school.

	Examined	Passed
Driver Petrol	134	116
Fabric Worker	54	54
Metal Rigger	108	76
Mates	1,612	1,375
Metal Worker	66	66
Class 'R' Reservist	53	53
AAF & SR Airmen	59	59

It is quite clear from these figures that the recently-introduced trade of mates was most in demand. While there is little information about the exact role, it is assumed that they supported other tradesmen in doing the more simple and routine tasks, leaving the skilled airmen to do the more complex jobs. At the same time the mate would be gain experience on the job, and learn from his fellow tradesmen, so that in a short while he would become qualified to complete any job that came along.

As well as the figures quoted above, it was confirmed in the statistics that, of the 2,141 trainees who had taken examinations and trade tests, 2063 passed. The total strength of the unit at the end of December 1935 was 1,337, with 194 instructors and 79 civilian members of staff. The total number of movements, including postings, was 5,580.

In January 1936, owing to the significant number of trainee engine and airframe fitters, the SoTT found that there was a shortage of service and civilian instructors—temporary arrangements had to be made to cope with the situation. As a stop-gap measure, a further number of civilians were employed as instructors on a probationary period of three months. An additional section was also established, with four squadrons for drill and any other matters, except for technical training. An extra officer was allocated for that purpose.

The School of Air Navigation was formed at Manston on 6 January, as an amalgamation of the Air Navigation School at Andover and the Navigation School that had been based at RAF Calshot. It was responsible for air navigation and the training of general reconnaissance pilots—the main type of training that they undertook was known as the 'N' Course. The school was under the control of the Air Officer Commander of Inland Area, who received his orders directly from the Air Ministry.

Seeing as both No. 48 Squadron and the School of Air Navigation were involved in the training of navigation and general reconnaissance crews, the CO of No. 48 Squadron took his orders from the CO of the School of Air Navigation. That post was filled by Wing Commander G. H. Harrison DSC, who had served with Middlesex Regiment during the First World War. On 23 January 1917, still only in the rank of 2nd Lieutenant, he had been seconded to the Royal Flying Corps. Eighteen months later he had held the rank of Captain; the award of his DSC had been announced in *RAF Communique* No. 17, which covered the period 22–28 July 1918.

A number of buildings had to be turned into makeshift barracks in order to accommodate all the airmen and officers at the school. Even one which had previously served as a church was commandeered. A small number of buildings were quickly erected, but not all of those who arrived at Manston appreciated their new surroundings—whether they had been recently built or not.

LAC Turner had served with the Air Navigation School at Andover, and said that it had been a happy place. Manston, however, was not to his liking. He described it as a typical training camp, an awkward place for full-blown regulars, with awful food and harsh discipline—certainly harsher than it had been at Andover. Soon after he arrived he was put on a charge for having a dirty hairbrush, but fortunately it was admonished by his CO. For LAC. Turner, Manston's only redeeming quality was that he had an aunt who lived locally, and he took the opportunity to visit her and enjoy her good home cooking.

When it was formed at Manston, the School of Air Navigation was equipped with three SARO Clouds and six Avro (626) Prefects, the latter being a rare beast, with only a small number in RAF Service. The Prefect had first flown in 1930, and was a biplane powered by an Armstrong Siddley Lynx 240-hp engine. Although many of those produced for service in the Egyptian and Brazilian air forces had three cockpits, those in RAF service—for training navigators and reconnaissance pilots—only had two. The Prefect was almost identical to the Avro Tutor, and had been designed by Roy Chadwick—who would later go on to design the Avro Lancaster. However, unlike that famous bomber, only 198 were ever built, and only a small number of British service personnel ever flew it.

A number of instructors at the School of Air Navigation were civilians—mainly experienced former air force or naval officers who had retired from the service. One of them was retired Capt. Bertie Arthur Millson DSC DFC. Capt. Millson had been awarded his Royal Aero Club Certificate, No. 3425, in August 1916, and had served with both No. 7 and No. 7a Squadrons—which had operated out of Manston in 1917. The unit had been part of No. 3 Wing, which operated Handley Page O/100s. In January 1917 Millson had been injured while ferrying one of them (serial number 1464) to France, when it crash-landed near Dunkirk.

On the night of 3–4 October 1917 Capt. Millson had flown two sorties to attack an important railway junction. While all the other crews had flown at a minimum height of 4,000 feet, to try and avoid the intense anti-aircraft fire, he flew down to 800 feet to ensure his bombs reached their target. He was awarded with the DFC for his actions on that night, and for his record of sixty-four sorties over enemy-held territory at night. This was reported in the *London Gazette* on 17 April 1918. He was forty-two years old by the time he became an instructor, but what he lacked in youth he made up for with his vast experience.

January 1936 was a busy month at Manston. No. 500 Squadron began to get rid of their now ancient Vickers Virginias, and replaced them with the Hawker Hart—which was powered by a single 525-hp Rolls-Royce Kestrel engine. Sadly the light day-bomber was already outdated, and its top speed of 180 mph and maximum 500-lb bomb load were no match for the aircraft being developed by potential enemy forces.

The Hart was totally outclassed, especially compared to the Hawker Hurricane, which flew for the first time on 6 November 1935, and the Supermarine Spitfire, which was test-flown at the beginning of March 1936. The only thing that the Hart had in common with the Hurricane was that both types had been designed by Sydney Camm. It is likely that the only reason that No. 500 Squadron was equipped with the Hart was that it was a special reserve unit rather than a regular squadron. Ironically, one of the most modern types of aircraft was also about to enter service at Manston.

In March 1936 No. 48 Squadron was re-equipped with the Avro Anson, a revolutionary new type of aircraft that was powered by two Armstrong Siddeley Cheetah 350-hp engines. The Anson had originally been built as a

Empire Air Day 1936. This visitor was allowed access to the cockpit of a Saro Cloud from No. 48 Squadron. (*Kent Library Services*)

Empire Air Day 1936. Inside the cockpit of the Saro Cloud, with the visitor being shown the controls. (*Kent Library Services*)

civil aircraft; Imperial Airways had ordered two of them as early as 1934, but that order had later been cancelled. The prototype for the RAF, K4771, had been built at Avro's factory in Newton Heath and assembled at Chadderton, where the mighty Lancaster would be built four years later. The Anson had first flown in April 1935, with the Air Ministry initially unconvinced that it was what they wanted—however, its capabilities in general reconnaissance and maritime roles were eventually recognised.

The first batch of sixty Ansons, serial numbers K6152 to K6211, were delivered to the RAF between March 1936 and April 1937. It was the first monoplane to be entered into RAF service with a retractable undercarriage, which was raised manually by the turn of a wheel in the cabin. It took about 140 turns of a crank handle to fully retract the wheels, and for short flights this was not worth the effort—however, despite the extra drag reducing the aircraft's air-speed by about 30 mph, the Anson still had enough power to outrun many of the other planes in the RAF's service.

A wonderful photograph exists of No. 48 Squadron's Ansons, showing them lined up on the airfield with their pilots standing by, waiting to be inspected. Although the date it was taken is not known, it was almost certainly in 1936. In the foreground is Anson K6158, code letter 'E', and next to that is K6173, code letter 'C'. K6159, code letter 'X', is the last one that can be clearly identified, but there are sixteen Ansons in the photo altogether. In the background there are three SARO Clouds, on the eastern side of the airfield,

A line up of Avro Ansons from No. 48 Squadron, with K6158 in foreground. (*Author's collection via Ron Collier*)

looking quite neglected. The Anson would be around for a very long time, and the first few units to be equipped with the type were formed at Manston.

No. 48 Squadron was equipped with two high-speed launches to assist in its role of general reconnaissance and search and rescue. They were powered by ancient aero engines that had not been very well-maintained, and it was generally noted that the engines stopped working after about fifteen minutes. On one occasion they were required for a vital operation, however, and they managed to hold out long enough for their crews to rescue a number of yachtsmen from the Royal Temple Yacht Club.

The club, which is based in Ramsgate, had organised a race around Goodwin Sands. When a squall suddenly blew up many of the yachts were grounded on quicksand, thereby placing their crews in danger. Commanding Officer Wg Cdr Bryson heard about what had happened through a wireless telegram message that was sent to the station—he despatched the two boats immediately, without hesitation. There were doubts about the serviceability of the engines in the launches, but they did not let their crews down—they managed to pull the yachts off the sand. The members of the yacht club were extremely grateful, and made Grp Capt. Strugnell and Wg Cdr Bryson honorary life-members by way of thanks.

There were also further developments on the civil side during the beginning of 1936, when fuel and customs facilities became available at Ramsgate Airport. The Thanet Aero Club was established at the airport, with the main instructors being John Banting (as chief instructor), Cliff Gifford, and Ken Clarke. Its first aeroplane was a de Havilland Hornet Moth, G-ADMM, but within a short while it would be equipped with a number of Miles Hawk Trainers and DH 87s.

The trial of Hermann Görtz began at the Old Bailey on Wednesday 4 March 1936, with Justice Greaves-Lord presiding. Mr J. D. Cassels MC and Mr Eustace Fulton prosecuted for the Crown, while Görtz was defended by Mr R. P. Croom-Johnson KC and Mr Alexander Cairn. Görtz pleaded not guilty. The circumstances of the defendant's arrival in Britain were mentioned, along with how he had rented the bungalow in Broadstairs from Mrs Johnson. Mrs Johnson's concern over the German's quick departure was detailed, in addition to the postcard he had sent promising his return. There were many twist and turns, including an appeal for the postponement of the trial so that witnesses could be brought from Germany. Ironically, the material supplied by Kenneth Lewis was not considered to be in breach of the Official Secrets Act.

Evidence included a letter that Görtz had written to the German Air Ministry, stating that he had been an intelligence officer during the First World War and that he had successfully interrogated a number of British airmen. It was also later claimed that he had served alongside Hitler's deputy, Hermann Göring. Görtz had argued that he considered himself suitable for employment in the intelligence services, and there was an unsigned letter saying that he would place himself at the disposal of the secret service. A letter was found from the German Air Minister, dated 29 January 1935, saying that he regretted that he could not employ Görtz. When questioned on his application to join the German intelligence service, Görtz denied everything and argued that he was hoping to be appointed as an air attaché in Washington.

With a wife and three children in Germany, Görtz needed money to pay off the £500 debt that he owed to a company in Hamburg. He had worked for Siemens, in his capacity as a lawyer, from 1929–31, and he claimed they had failed to pay him wages amounting to £7,500. Görtz also asserted that he had travelled to England to avoid his creditors, and that he had hoped to write a book about the Royal Air Force. This, he argued, was why he had been gathering material in East Anglia and Manston.

Despite Görtz's pleas to the court that he was innocent, the jury found him guilty on Monday 9 March. He was sentenced to four years of penal servitude, to be served out in Maidstone Prison. The press gave very little coverage to the case or the verdict; most newspapers lead with stories about the deteriorating international situation, covering Germany's activities in the Rhineland and Anthony Eden's speech on Britain's obligation to defend Belgium and France. Görtz's activities had not gone unnoticed in Germany, and many of those in the intelligence services admired his dedication to the fatherland. However, Görtz would have to serve his sentence before they could put him to any further use.

7

Aviation in Thanet

In 1936 the Member of Parliament for Thanet was Captain Harold Harington Balfour MC, and he made the news in April when he became a pupil at the newly-formed Ramsgate Flying Club. On Saturday 7 April the former Royal Flying Corps pilot decided to renew his flying skills, having flown with Nos 43 and 60 Squadron—when he was credited with destroying nine enemy aircraft.

By the end of the war he had reached the rank of Major, but he had left the RAF in 1923 with the rank of Captain. He had served in a number of posts at the Air Ministry before being elected as the MP for Thanet in 1929. Capt. Balfour claimed that his reason for becoming a pupil at Ramsgate was that he had heard it was equipped with the very latest equipment for the purpose of flying instruction, of which he had no experience.

On the day in question he was one of fourteen pupils awaiting tuition, and was taken flying by Flight Lieutenant Eckersley Maslin. After a short flight around the airfield Capt. Balfour took over the controls and made several landings, later admitting that it was a novel experience for him to be a pupil. He also said that he was considering an offer to become president of Ramsgate Flying Club. It seems that the true purpose of him becoming a pupil was something of a publicity stunt.

In April 1936 the role of No. 500 Squadron transformed from being a Special Reserve Squadron into an Auxiliary Air Force unit. Fred Wilson and other aircraftmen on the squadron were given a letter from the Commanding Officer, informing them of the changes and explaining what it meant for the members. It stated:

It is desired to point out to all Special Reserve ranks of the Unit, that now this Squadron is to all intents and purposes an Auxiliary Air Force Unit, the great importance of regular attendance.

Upon their keenness and regular attendance will depend the whole efficiency of No. 500 (B) Squadron, for unless the Squadron is run by

Auxiliary Personnel at week-ends etc., the whole object of an A.A.F. Squadron has been defeated.

From 30 April the evening work roster was rearranged and, in addition to duty at weekends, the duty hours on Thursdays and Fridays were now 5.30 p.m. to 8.15 p.m. It was to be accepted, at the discretion of the CO, that airmen whose work was some distance from the station would be allowed to start their duty later and extend their duty time. It was made clear that airmen should not put off attending for duty just because they might arrive later than the scheduled hours.

The development of No. 500 as an auxiliary unit coincided with another change of command, when Squadron Leader Lawson was posted out to the staff of HQ Middle East in April. His replacement was Flt Lt Walter George Woolliams, who had served with No. 39 Squadron at Spittlegate as a young Pilot Officer. In November 1927 he had moved to No. 99 Squadron at Bircham Newton, and had then been promoted to Squadron Leader in February 1932.

In May of that year Flt Lt Woolliams had been posted to No. 500 Squadron's sister unit No. 501 (City of Bristol) Squadron, based at Filton, meaning that he would have visited Manston on a number of previous occasions. However, in October 1932 he had been posted overseas, serving with No. 70 Squadron and on staff duty in Transjordan and Palestine; his posting to the home establishment and No. 500 Squadron must have been quite welcome. A short time after taking over command, Woolliams was awarded a permanent commission with the rank of Flight Lieutenant.

April also saw the recommencement of training for metal riggers. There had been a brief interlude caused by a shortage of instructors, but they were in high demand due to the rapid expansion of the RAF. The numbers of pupils that the school and RAF Manston could cope with and accommodate was about to reach in its peak.

Whatever the situation, as on most other RAF stations, there was always time for fun and games, although some might have thought that the occasional prank went too far. One such incident involved Wg Cdr Bryson, who nearly fell afoul of one of his young fellow officers after he had been jilted by his girlfriend. The wing commander was in the ante-room of the officers' mess when the officer suddenly appeared with a revolver, and began to shoot out the face of the clock. It is not known what happened to the young officer, but given the circumstances it is likely that he was given a strict dressing down by the CO, Group Captain Strugnell, and ordered to buy a new clock! Most of the officers and airmen had experienced similar emotional turmoil at one time or another, and so might have felt sorry for the young officer.

On another occasion, some members of an auxiliary squadron decided to relieve their boredom one evening by playing skittles in the corridor of the

Rigger Aircraftman Fred Wilson, standing outside the mess with his two colleagues reading the papers. Note the medal ribbon on Fred Wilson's tunic, and that of the corporal sitting on the left. (*John Wilson*)

Another group of airmen from No. 500 Squadron casually posing for a photo, with Fred Wilson third from left. Note the airman second from the right, who is wearing many medal ribbons. (*John Wilson*)

mess. As they did not have any actual skittles, they decided to improvise and use the nearest thing to hand—chamber pots, of which there was a plentiful supply. When the President of the Mess Committee arrived the next morning, he was greeted with a pile of broken pottery, and worked out a rough estimate of sixty broken chamber pots. Being a resourceful chap, the PMC worked out the cost to replace them and multiplied that by three, before presenting the bill to the squadron concerned. Not only did the unit pay up, but members of the squadron went out and bought a lot of beautifully hand-painted chamber pots, which were then ceremoniously presented to the mess.

There were a number of serious accidents in 1936, and one of the first involved a Hawker Audax of No. 2 Squadron, K1995, on Saturday 23 May, at Holywell, near Hawkinge. In November 1935 the unit had moved out of Manston to Hawkinge, but although the squadron was not based at Manston anymore there are a number of good reasons for including the incident in this account.

Flying Officer Paul Wingrave Ashton was a well-known sportsman in Thanet, who played rugby and boxed at a light-heavyweight level. He was the pilot of the Hawker Audax in the accident, which occurred on Empire Air Day at Hawkinge—a major event. The crash happened out of sight of the crowd, but the aircraft hit some power cables and caused a blackout in Dover which lasted for a number of hours. Also on board the Audax was Leading Aircraftman Joseph Henry Simpson, who was also a member of No. 2 Squadron. Wingrave Ashton died in the crash.

Born in South Africa, Fg Off. Wingrave Ashton had graduated from RAF Cranwell in 1934, where he had been an outstanding pupil. On 4 September 1934, it was announced in *The London Gazette* that he had been awarded a permanent commission, with his seniority dating from 28 July. He had been posted to Manston with No. 2 Squadron in July 1934, and was promoted to the rank of Flying Officer on 28 January—just four months before he was killed.

On the day of the accident, Fg Off. Wingrave Ashton's aircraft was one of three that had made a mock attack on a wooden fort, which had been constructed in the middle of the airfield. LACW Simpson, the passenger, was described as an air gunner, and it is not known why he was on board. The crash occurred just after the Audax had made its pass on the mock fort. The accident happened out of sight of the crowd, and many spectators thought that the noise and smoke from the crash was part of the show. What had really happened was that Wingrave's Audax had flown into some power cables, and crashed to the ground in flames. Five out of the seven overhead power cables had been severed, which severely affected the power supply in Dover and the surrounding area.

The *Isle of Thanet Gazette* reported the incident with the headline, 'Air Day Tragedy: Flying Officer Ashton's Fatal Crash'. It described an incident it claimed was still being talked about in sporting circles—when Wingrave Ashton had flown back from a tough rugby game at Leicester, exhausted, but still insisted on boxing in a tournament that had been previously arranged. His opponent was heavier than him, but he still won the fight, being cheered on loudly by the crowd—most of whom knew what he had been through. Wingrave Ashton had played rugby for both the station and the RAF Service team, and when he left Manston for Hawkinge he had been very much missed. He was a popular officer amongst his fellow officers and those in the ranks, and his tragic death was mourned by all.

June was a busy month, with No. 206 Squadron reformed at Manston with the Avro Anson that had been supplied by 'C' Flight of No. 48 Squadron. The squadron had been equipped with the DH 9 during the First World War, when it had been based in France and Egypt. Originally being No. 6 (Royal Naval Air Service) Squadron, it had been re-numbered No. 206 in April, after the formation of the RAF. It was commanded by Wing Commander Francis John Vincent DFC who had recently returned from serving as Air Staff at HQ Middle East. Having joined the service at the end of the First World War, Vincent had served as a Flight Commander on a home defence at Great Yarmouth. He had later commanded No. 56 Squadron in 1925, and No. 84 Squadron in 1927. No. 206 Squadron was the second unit to have been formed at Manston in just over a month, but its time at the station would be quite short.

On 20 June an 'Aviation Service' was held in Canterbury Cathedral, and RAF Manston provided one officer and 260 airmen to form a guard of honour. Sir Philip Sassoon, the Secretary of State for Air, presented two ensigns to the Cathedral at the service, one to represent the RAF and another to represent civil aviation. The RAF ensign was dedicated by the Archbishop of Canterbury, and then hung up on the wall. A special church parade service was also held in Thanet, where the RAF presented a standard to the members of the Thanet branch of the Comrades of the Royal Air Force's Association.

There was another serious accident on 25 June, involving an Avro Anson of No. 48 Squadron, K6166—but it was one that fortunately did not involve the loss of life. Plt Off. R. A. Atkins was flying out at sea, 6 miles off the coast of Tankerton, and was in the process of changing over fuel tanks from the main tank to the emergency tank. At some point during the procedure both Armstrong Siddley Cheetah engines began to splutter and fail, leaving Atkins to circle around and 'pancake' onto the sea. Rather ironically, the rescue was triggered by the crew of a German airliner, on their way to Croydon, who saw the Anson in the water.

Aircraft from Manston and lifeboats from Ramsgate and Broadstairs joined in the search. The Margate lifeboat was just about to be launched when news broke that the aircraft had been found. Atkins had fortunately escaped with little more than a few minor facial injuries, and he managed to scramble out onto the wing. He was soon spotted by Mr J. Heathcote in his motorboat *Indian Chief*, which was based in Herne Bay, and he managed to climb aboard the boat's dinghy.

Atkins was amongst a small number of officers who had been posted to No. 48 Squadron directly from the RAF College at Cranwell on 14 December 1935, and was awarded a permanent commission. K6166 was from the first batch of Ansons to be delivered to the RAF, and it was only the fifteenth aircraft to enter service. It is believed that this was the first Anson to be lost, and this fact would not have gone down well with the Air Officer Commanding. There is no doubt that the pilot's inexperience would have been questioned during the subsequent Board of Inquiry. It is not known what happened to the young Pilot Officer, but in *Flight* magazine for 20 July 1939 there is a mention of a 'Flying Officer R. A. Atkins' being promoted to the rank of Flight Lieutenant—this may well be the same officer.

Over the summer of 1936 there were a number of different aviation shows and events held around Thanet. One of the first was held on Monday 27 July at Richborough. Though technically not in Thanet, Richborough is just a short distance from Manston, and during the First World War its port had been built to ferry supplies and heavy equipment to the army in France. Known as the 'Secret Port', Richborough already had a long and renowned history—just a few hundred yards across the marshes is Richborough Castle, which was built by the Romans in the 1st century AD.

The air show at Richborough was promoted with the slogan 'Flying For All', and the display, which had been organised by a Mr C. W. A. Scott, promised three hours of classic flying and entertainment in two shows. It involved a dazzling display of aerobatics by a Tiger Moth flown by Mr Idwal Jones, who was known as the Welsh Wizard. Mrs Crossley, a British airwoman and pilot, also featured, and the *East Kent Times* claimed that she was the first woman to enter the ranks of aerobatic pilots. There was a display of parachuting by Mr Harris, and gliding by Miss Joan Meakin—an accomplished glider pilot. The 'Flying Flea' and the Autogiro were also displayed at Richborough, and over the next few weeks they would appear again at other events in the area.

The 3-mile open team event of the RAF Championships was held at RAF Uxbridge on Friday 17 July. Despite the efforts of Aircraftman A. H. Reeve, the team from RAF Manston only finished third. RAF Henlow, the championship holders, were forced into second place by RAF Halton. Reeve had completed the first mile in five minutes and one second, two miles in ten minutes and five seconds, and completed the individual event in fifteen minutes and seven seconds. In the event held earlier in the week Reeve had only finished third.

8

Preparing For War

While the people of Thanet watched and enjoyed the various air shows during the summer of 1936, the structure of the RAF was changing. Some of the changes affected units at RAF Manston and, in particular, No. 3 School of Technical Training. On 10 July it became part of the newly formed No. 24 'Training' Group, which was to be based at RAF Halton. RAF Halton ceased to exist as an independent command, and became HQ No. 24 'Training' Group.

Also on the 10th, the School of Air Navigation and No. 48 Squadron were transferred to No. 23 'Training' Group, which had been transferred to training command in May. On the grander scale these changes were quite trivial, compared to what would happen just a few days later.

At 11.59 p.m. on 13 July 1936 the Air Defence of Great Britain, which had been formed in 1925, was abolished and replaced by a new structure that would prepare Britain for any future conflict. At midnight RAF Fighter Command was formed, with its headquarters at Stanmore. The new command absorbed No. 11 Group Fighter Command, No. 22 Group—with its army co-operation units—and the Royal Observer Corps. Bomber Command was formed under Air Marshal Sir John Steel. With its HQ at Uxbridge, it took control of Nos 1, 2, and 3 Group Bomber Command and No. 6 Auxiliary Group. Coastal Command was also formed, with its HQ at Lee-on Solent; its Commander-in-Chief was AM Arthur Murray Longmore.

Another major development concerning the RAF came when Viscount Swinton (Philip Lloyd Greame), the Secretary of State for Air, informed the House of Lords about the formation of the Royal Air Force Reserve. Volunteers would receive flying training at weekends and during annual fifteen-day summer camps, and they would have to serve for a minimum period of five years.

The RAFVR was formed to supplement the Auxiliary Air Force that had been established in 1925, and it had been preceded by an organisation called the Reserve of Royal Air Force Officers (RAFO). Initially RAFVR officers were civilians recruited from reserve flying schools, which were run by a civil contractor that largely employed members of the RAFO. Members of the RAFO were normally officers who were qualified as pilots and had spent four years on short service commissions.

The main difference between the RAFVR and the AAF was that the former was organised around individual officers, whereas the latter was organised around squadrons—with each unit being allocated a number that began with six. Each unit was also associated with a particular town or city; the first one to be formed had been No. 600 'City of London' Squadron, at Northolt in October 1925.

Despite only having been formed at Manston that June, at the end of July No. 206 Squadron departed the station under the command of Wing Commander Vincent, and was posted to Bircham Newton in Norfolk. It remained equipped with the Avro Anson until March 1940, when it received the Lockheed Hudson—by that time, it was operating from St Eval in Cornwall. With an octopus as the symbol on its badge, and its motto being 'Naught Escape Us', No. 206 Squadron was to continue in service for many more years, later becoming one of the first units to receive the mighty Nimrod.

Even with the increasing tension and the changes being made to the structure of the RAF, things continued to go on as normal. Over the bank holiday weekend of 2–3 August an air race was held at Ramsgate Airport. It was an event described by *Aeroplane* magazine as a 'Flying Flea fest at Ramsgate'. Designed by Frenchman Henri Mignet, the original Flea had been designated as the H. M. 14 and had a wing span of just 17 feet, with a small but roomy cabin. It was first built in 1920, and between 1929 and 1933 Mignet developed several prototypes that he had test-flown in fields near Soissons.

In the French language the Flea was also known as the 'Pou du Ciel', which translates into English as the 'Flying Flea'. Its original engine was a two-stroke 17-hp Aubier-Dunne motorcycle engine, which gave it a top speed of 62 mph. The main version of the Flea demonstrated at Ramsgate in 1936 was the H. M. 18. When empty it weighed 250 lbs. It had a lightweight fixed undercarriage with no brakes, and had been designed so that the air flow from the engine was directed at the tail—making its rudder very effective and easily able to turn on the ground. Between 1935 and 1936 the aerodynamics and engine of the Flea had undergone a series of redevelopments by a number of English airmen, and as a result the Fleas which arrived at Ramsgate were totally different from one another.

A week or two before the race was held there had scarcely been any entries, and the organisers feared that there might be no Fleas to race. Of those that had arrived, some of the machines—particularly the French ones—had no registrations. Furthermore, there were a number of other problems concerning handicapping, because the powers of their different types of engines were not known.

Apart from the Fleas, however, there was a rally of other aeroplanes of various types, including a Short Scion flown by Mr D. R. Pobjoy and a

Hornet Moth flown by Mr W. M. C. Peatfield, who was a pupil at Ramsgate Flying School. There was also a Hilson Praga, a Swallow, an Aeronica, and a Cierva Autogiro flown by Mr Reginald Brie, but the highlight of the event was reported to be the Flying Flea Race.

In the end there were seven entries, including Mr Appleby's Flea, which was the first British-made machine fitted with a Carden engine. Mr E. Bret represented France, with an Ava four-cylinder two-stroke engine, along with Mr R. Robineau and Mr J. Colli. Machines flown by Mr C. A. Oscroft and Flight Lieutenant A. E. Clousten also represented Britain. The race was won by Mr Bret, who claimed the £100 cash prize and a silver trophy. Mr Mignet's new machine, designated the H.M. 18 Cabin Flea, won the prize for the best appearance and equipment. On the tail of the aircraft Mr. Mignet had inscribed: 'The Flying Flea flies In England. I Thank British Air Ministry'. The inscription was a reference to the fact that the Flea had been temporarily grounded after a serious accident at Penshurt in May, and had not been allowed to fly again until wind tunnel tests were carried out.

Fg Off. Frank Donald Nugent (34013) was posted to Manston to take command of the Practice Flight on 4 August 1936. It was equipped with a Westland Wallace, K8676. In May 1935, when Nugent had qualified as a probationary Pilot Officer, *Flight* magazine had published his name as 'Pilot Officer Frank Ronald Nugent'—in June's copy it printed his real name, and an apology. The Practice Flight unit had gone through a few changes over the years; in February 1930 it had been known as the 'Permanent Reception Flight'. Back then its role had been to guide visiting aircraft into Manston, and also to get airborne and recognise unidentified aircraft flying in the vicinity of the airfield.

In 1936 the unit was still being called the Practice Flight and, although it was not one of the Manston's most prestigious units, it counted a renowned sportsman amongst its ranks. Aircraftman 1st Class James Beugg, who played water polo and swam for the RAF, had been deliberately posted to the station so that he could use its facilities to train. He remained at Manston until 1939.

Another member of the small team of eight on the Practice Flight was LAC Stubbs, who at some point in 1936 was badly injured when he had been struck by a propeller. The main injuries were to his head and arms, with which he used to try and protect himself; he was lucky to have survived. By 1941 Fg Off. Frank Donald Nugent had been promoted to the rank of Squadron Leader. He retired in 1969 with the rank of Wing Commander, working for Airwork Training Services (Air Holdings) in Perth.

On Sunday 9 August, a week after the air race at Ramsgate Airport, there was another event held at Manston to celebrate Empire Air Day—which had taken place at many RAF stations earlier that year, in May. The event was widely advertised in local newspapers such as the *East Kent Times,* which described T. C. Campbell as the main attraction. In 1934 he had been known as the man who crossed the world in four days in the England–Australia race, and now he was chosen to present Empire Day itself.

It was claimed that the purpose of the event was twofold: first of all, to demonstrate the reliability of British aircraft, with no fewer than twelve machines exhibited. Secondly, it aimed to encourage a greater and wider interest in aviation by giving the public an opportunity to experience air travel at a minimal cost. The event was widely advertised in the local press, promising a 'really wonderful display of aerobatics & crazy flying by Empire's star pilots'. It was to begin at 2 p.m. and finish at dusk. Amongst the main attractions were the Flying Fleas and a wonderful display of parachutists, who were to drop both individually and in mass formation. Admission was 1 shilling for adults or 6 pence for children, and the entrance fee for cars was 1 shilling.

Also appearing at the Empire Air Day display were Miss Pauline Gower and Miss Dorothy Spicer, described by the local press as 'brilliant young airwomen'. These women had joined together to become the first female airline operators. Miss Gower held a pilot's 'B' Licence, a wireless telegraphy-operator's licence, and a valuable and much sought-after certificate for navigation—as well as certificates for blind and instrument flying. She had flown with a total of 20,000 passengers, without losing a single one of them or being involved in an accident. The *East Kent Times* claimed that Miss Spicer had been born with a proverbial golden spanner in her mouth—she was the only fully-qualified female ground engineer in the world.

Unfortunately the event was not without incident. During one demonstration two of the parachutists came close to losing their lives after they collided in the air. It was reported in the newspaper as 'MID AIR COLLISION: Thrilling scenes at Ramsgate Airport'. The two men involved were Mr Bill Hire—a local man, attached to the staff of Ramsgate Airport as a parachute trainer—and Mr Bruce Williams. T. C. Campbell had been unable to find a second parachutist to take part in a parachute race with Mr Williams, and Bill Hire volunteered his services so the crowd wouldn't be disappointed. He had performed at various events over the summer, including a parachute jump at the recent Flying Flea Festival.

The two men made the double jump at approximately 2,000 feet, leaping from different aeroplanes. However, they collided almost immediately and both of their parachutes collapsed. Bruce Williams' legs had somehow struck the side of Bill Hire's parachute, and it was claimed that both men fell like stones for over 1,000 feet, before finally recovering at no more than 700 feet above the ground. Both men were wrenching at the rigging lines to try and free themselves, and whether by an act of God or a gust of wind, suddenly both parachutes became separated again.

The crowd was stricken with an awful silence. The commentator was praised for his calm and professional talk over the microphone, which was described as being quite unemotional and without a trace of excitement. Both men made what were described as heavy landings, but they released their harnesses and walked away from the scene without any fuss—despite the fact that they had come within an inch of losing their lives.

'Manston is Busy', stated a headline in the *East Kent Times* in August. It went on to say:

> The Royal Air Force Expansion Scheme has been responsible for extraordinary activity at Manston Camp this year, and the School of Technical Training is working at high pressure.
>
> A new squadron, No. 206 (General Reconnaissance) was formed at Manston in June, and has been drafted to another station. Like No. 48 Squadron, formed at Manston earlier in the year, it is equipped with the speedy Avro Anson monoplane.
>
> No Army co-operation work has been undertaken at Manston this year, as in previous summers, although Territorials have been in camp a few hundred yards from the hangars.

During the autumn of 1936, No. 48 Squadron and the School of Air Navigation continued to be build up their strength with officers and airmen being posted to the units on an almost weekly basis. Squadron Leader G. H. Harrison DFC and Pilot Officers C. D. S Smith and A. E. Williamson were posted in during September. Flt Lt R. H. Harris, Fg Off. J. E. Allen, Fg Off. Thresher, and Plt Off. St J. Thomson were amongst the officers posted in during October.

There was another change of command for No. 500 Squadron in October, when Sqn Ldr Craven Goring Hohler took over from Flt Lt Woolliams. Hohler joined the AAF in 1932, but had resigned from that commission in November 1935 in order to join the Regular Air Force. He was promoted to the rank of Squadron Leader and awarded a permanent commission in that rank from 20 October 1936.

With a name like Goring it might have sounded like the squadron leader should have been serving in the Luftwaffe rather than the RAF, but he came from the village of Wrotham, in Kent, and had been educated at King's College, Cambridge. He was the son of Edward Theobald and Agnes Veneitia Hohler—Goring was his mother's maiden name.

Also during October a foreign visitor arrived to look around No. 3 SoTT, thereby adding to the number of Romanian, Japanese, and Mexican officers who had previously toured its workshops. The visit on the 9th was from Colonel Chang-Tsu-Chien, the liaison officer from the Chinese army.

Football was always a popular sport, especially amongst airmen serving in the ranks. It was during this period that RAF Manston's football team was playing in the Kent Amateur League Eastern Section. Other teams in the league included Dover, Ramsgate Grenville, Chartham Mental Hospital, and Betteshanger Colliery. RAF Manston had finished the 1935–36 season in ninth place (out of a league made up of only twelve teams), after winning only six out of the twenty games played. They fared no better in November, with Dover beating them 5–1 on the 7th of that month.

On 11 December King Edward VIII abdicated the throne, shaking the world beyond Manston. He had been crowned on 20 January 1936 and had reigned for less than a year, but his affair with Mrs Wallace Simpson meant that he had little choice but to step down. Following his resignation he was given the title of Duke of Windsor, with his brother later being crowned as George VI.

By the end of 1936 no fewer than 4,560 pupils had passed through No. 3 SoTT, of whom over 3,000 had trained as mates. The complete breakdown was as follows:

	Examined	Passed
'A' Officers		
Parachute	171	170
Reserve Training	9	9
'B' Airmen		
Driver Petrol	359	290
Fabric Worker	80	80
Fitter AE	468	491
Metal Rigger	104	102
Metal Worker	3	3
Mate	3,373	3,441
Naval Ratings-Fabric	1	1
Parachute	26	25
AAF & ASR	43	43
Aircraft Welding (*Airmen*)	5	5
Aircraft Welding (*Royal Navy*)	1	1

At the end of December 1936 there were actually 1,647 airmen undergoing training, with a permanent staff force of 167 service personnel, in addition to 108 civilian instructors and their staff. Consequently, the total strength of No. 3 SoTT was 1,922.

These figures represent a huge increase in the number of pupils examined in 1935, with a 150% increase in the number of those who trained as mates. It is no wonder that the station was bursting at the seams and that it had been necessary to establish tented accommodation on the airfield.

Parachuting is best associated with No. 1 Parachute Training School (Central Landing School), which was established at Manchester Airport (Ringway) in June 1940. It is interesting, however, that No. 3 SoTT was already training officers and airmen of the RAF, as well as other services, in parachuting techniques, several years before the unit at Manchester was created. It is just another example of how RAF Manston was at the forefront of military training.

On 1 January 1937, the strength of HQ RAF Manston came in at 103 Regular Air Force officers and 2,188 airmen. Group Captain Strugnell remained as the Commanding Officer, with Sqn Ldr F. Wright on Adjutant duties.

In the 7 January 1937 issue of *Flight* magazine, an advert appeared for a book called *Martin's Air Navigation*, which claimed to be a concise guide to be used by those taking their 2nd Class Navigator's Licence. The book was published by C. W. Martin (RNAS & RAF), who claimed to be the chief instructor at the School of Air Navigation. Some potential students may have assumed that the school to which the book referred was the one based at Manston and run by the RAF, but they would have been wrong. In fact, there was no connection—the Empire Air Navigation School was based in Notting Hill High Street, London. It is unclear whether or not the author was deliberately trading under the RAF School of Navigation's name; there were no trading standards in those days!

In the same edition of *Flight* there was an advert which sought to recruit officers between the ages of eighteen to twenty-five for the RAFR. Applicants had to have a school certificate that was approved by the Oxford and Cambridge Board, and had to be of a good physique. The first year of service was a full-time commitment, but after completing their training reserve officers would only have to attend for twenty-four days each year. Each officer would have to serve for a minimum of five years.

January was a largely uneventful month at Manston, but February proved more interesting—starting with the 1 February formation of No. 224 Squadron from a cadre of No. 48 Squadron. No. 224 Squadron's association with Manston was brief and on the 15th the unit moved out to Boscombe Down, where it remained until July 1937.

On the 22nd there was a second fatal accident involving an Avro Anson; K6158 crashed at Ewell Minis near Dover, killing the three airmen on board and seriously injuring a fourth crew member. This was the fifth serious accident involving the Avro Anson since it had been introduced with No. 48 Squadron, the first one being K6166 in June 1936. The three other aircraft involved in the accidents came from No. 220 Squadron, based at Bircham Newton; No. 5 Flying Training School at Sealand; and No. 269 Squadron at Abbotsinch. Ironically, just a short time before the accident, K6158 had featured prominently in the foreground of a photo taken of No. 48 Squadron's Ansons, with the letter 'E' on its fuselage.

The Anson was being flown by Flt Lt George Edward Strangman and twenty-three-year-old Sergeant Pilot Maurice, from Neath, with twenty-six-year-old AC Stanley McCabe acting as the wireless operator. McCabe lived locally at 1 Granville Road, Ramsgate. Strangman survived the crash, but died in hospital two days later. The other officer on board, Flt Lt John Cooper, was seriously injured. The aircraft had taken off from Manston at 6.20 p.m. on a training flight; the pilots had unwittingly flown into some snow showers, which had quickly turned into a blizzard.

There was the possibility that the aircraft had been struck by lightning, and therefore it was thought that bad weather and a thunderstorm were to blame for the accident; the pilots would have been unable to maintain control of the Anson in such severe weather. Sergeant Pilot Gwilyn James Maurice was buried in Minster Cemetery.

On the same day that K6158 was lost No. 3 SoTT received another visitor to tour its workshops—Lt Okuda, from the Japanese Navy. Considering what was to happen just a short while later, one might question the decision to allow potential enemies to be given guided tours of such units. Japan had been at war with China since 1931, when they had invaded Manchuria. Just a year after Lt Okuda's visit, Japanese troops would be involved in one of the greatest-ever atrocities in war: the Rape of Nanking.

In February No. 500 Squadron began to re-equip with the Hawker Hind, a variant of the Hawker Hart which the unit had operated since early 1936. The main difference between the Hind and the Hart was the engine, and that the former had been fitted with a more powerful 640-hp Rolls Royce Kestrel V engine. The unit would not get rid of all of its Harts immediately, instead continuing to operate them for a further three months.

On 3 March a Bessonneau Hangar was erected on the north-west side of the airfield, near the Reception Flight. Bessonneau Hangars were temporary shelters that had been introduced during the First World War and designed by the company *Établissements Bessonneau*, which was run by Frenchman Julian Bessonneau. The hangars were mainly built of wood with metal supports, and were picketed to the ground with large metal pegs.

There were more foreign visitors to Manston on the 16th, when three French Air Force officers toured the workshops of No. 3 SoTT. The officers were Commander L. H. Amontlelay and Capt. M. S. P. Tourmemire, and they were accompanied by Lieutenant-Colonel P. T. G. Fournier.

A new establishment was issued for No. 3 SoTT on 1 April, when it was raised to 1,818 airmen who would be trained in various trades. On the 5th the Under Secretary of State for Air, Sir Philip Sassoon, visited Manston and toured the school, observing the airmen under instruction in all aspects of trade training.

The grave of twenty-four-year-old Sergeant Gwilyn James Maurice, from Neath, in Minster Cemetery. He was the pilot of Anson K6158, which crashed on 22 February 1937. (*John Williams*)

10 May was a proud day for RAF Manston, when CO Wing Commander Bryson, along with 200 non-commissioned officers and airmen from No. 3 SoTT, were sent to London on Coronation Duty. The Coronation of King George VI took place on 12 May in Westminster Abbey; Wg Cdr Bryson and Warrant Officer Beckett were amongst those awarded the Coronation Medal.

A couple of weeks later the air staff sent out a letter to thank all the RAF units who had been involved in the Coronation Parade. It expressed the appreciation of the Chief of General Imperial Staff Lord Cavan, and the Adjutant General of the Army, for the high standards shown by the RAF's contingent. The letter congratulated those who took part in the Coronation Parade and also officers and airmen who had been involved in the preliminary training. The letter appeared in command routine orders No. 217 of 27 May, and was to be repeated in routine orders on all stations and units.

There were a couple of air accidents in Thanet during June. The first involved a civilian aircraft flown by Mr Derek George Duval, a Margate businessman who lived in Birchington. He was about to buy a Tipsy S. 2, G-AEWJ, from a company based at Croydon Airport. On Sunday 6 June he spent the morning being shown the controls and flying around Ramsgate Airport with a demonstration pilot, in order for him to become familiar with the cockpit. Mr Duval had already gone solo, and made a number of successful take-offs and landings, when he took off for the last time, shortly after 2 p.m. When he was only 30 feet into the air, the aircraft suddenly nose-dived into a potato field.

Mr James Groombridge, who lived in Tabernacle Cottages, witnessed the accident and was first on the scene to help rescue Mr Duval—who was trapped in the cockpit. The nose of the aircraft was buried deep in the ground, and Mr Groombridge was aware that the petrol tank was unstable, but he was unable to release Mr Duval's due to the nature of his injuries. Fortunately, Mr Groombridge had the presence of mind to do something about it; with the help of a pair of wire cutters, he managed to hack and tear the petrol tank away from the remains of the cockpit. Meanwhile someone else had telephoned for an ambulance, which quickly arrived on the scene. Mr Duval was pulled from the wreckage and taken to Ramsgate Hospital, where he eventually recovered from his injuries.

On Friday 18 June, No. 48 Squadron lost another Anson when K8763 dived to the ground and crashed into an orchard near Leeds Castle. The aircraft had taken off from Manston at 9.46 p.m. on a night-training exercise, and it was carrying out low-level manoeuvres when it stalled. The only crew member on board the aircraft was twenty-six-year-old Sergeant Pilot William Hinson, who was killed outright. The accident was reported in *Flight* magazine on 1 July, which stated that the aircraft had crashed near a village in Leeds and confirmed that Sgt Hinson had lost his life. Hinson had joined the RAF in 1929, and had been flying since 1933.

9

Ramsgate in the Limelight

Ramsgate Airport was officially opened on 3 July 1937 by the Director of Civil Aviation, Sir Francis Shelmerdine CIE OBE FRAeS. It had already been open for two years, and in that time it had been transformed from a grass airfield, with barely any buildings or facilities, to an airport with a state-of-the-art building built in the art deco style.

The administrative and terminal building had been designed Mr. D. Pleydell Bouverie, and was built in the shape of an aircraft's wing—with a control tower at its centre. It was claimed that architects from all over the country had visited the airport to examine the building and its striking characteristics. The building was 125 feet long, 40 feet wide in the middle, and tapered out to 16 feet at both ends. A central corridor linked all the areas, such as the booking hall, club house, public lounge, a kitchen, and various offices.

The general contractors for the building's construction were a local firm: Grummant Brothers, based in Ramsgate. A number of other firms, such as Ellis and Ward Limited, came from London to carry out the electrical installation. The furniture was from a company called Finmar, and the glass from Vitrea Dawn Sheet Glass Company Limited. Both were also based in London. The contractor furthest away from Thanet was Saunders and Taylor Limited, who were based in Manchester—they installed the heating and hot water.

As it might have been predicted, the official opening attracted a large number of officials to Ramsgate. This included Lord Beaverbrook, who flew from London in a Lockheed 12 Junior Electra, G-AEMZ. Sir Francis Shelmerdine arrived in a Leopard Moth—he had departed from Croydon, but on his way there his motor car caught fire. Sir Francis and his wife escaped unharmed, but the incident might have acted as evidence that driving could be as dangerous as flying. He later apologised for arriving late, and joked that he had resorted to the 'antiquated form of locomotion known as a motor car'—which burst into flames while crossing Chelsea Bridge.

Lieutenant-Colonel Sir Francis Shelmerdine, the Director of Civil Aviation, and Alderman H. Stead, the Mayor of Ramsgate, looking over an aircraft at the official opening of Ramsgate Airport on 3 July 1937. (*Margate Museum*)

Mr Albert Batchelor in his Klemm Swallow. He had flown from the land which became Ramsgate Airport for many years before the airport opened. (*John Williams*)

Another view across Ramsgate Airport on the official opening day. Lord Beaverbrook's Lockheed Electra is taking off in the background, with a D.H. 84 Dragon and a D.H. 87 Hornet Moth also present. (*Margate Museum*)

The terminal building of Ramsgate Airport in its prime. (*Margate Museum*)

The original passenger terminal at Ramsgate Airport, from where passengers would depart for London. (*Margate Museum*)

Among those invited to the luncheon were the local MP for Thanet, Capt. H. H. Balfour; the Mayor of Ramsgate, Alderman H. Stead; the Deputy Mayor of Ramsgate, Alderman E. E. Dye; and Mr Whitney Straight. The guest list for the luncheon was arguably a 'who's-who' in local politics and aviation, and it seems that the main point of the official opening was a change in the airport's title. Whereas it had previously been called Ramsgate Airport (Aerodrome) it was now known as Ramsgate Municipal Airport.

Amongst those aircraft present and on display were a Spartan Cruiser (G-ACBM) and a D.H. 84 Dragon (G-AECZ), which belonged to the Straight Corporation. Also present were local aviator Albert Batchelor's B.A. Swallow (G-AERK), a Short Scion (G-AECU), and a D.H. 87 Hornet Moth (G-ADMM). Deck chairs were laid out in front of the terminal building, with just a simple wooden fence standing between the visitors and the aircraft on the airfield.

By 1937 Ramsgate Airport's director, Mr Whitney Straight, could add aircraft manufacturing to his extensive list of managerial skills and talents— he had built his own aircraft, designated the Miles Whitney Straight M.11. The aircraft was powered by a 130-hp Gipsy Major engine, and had actually been designed by Frederick George Miles of the Miles Aircraft Company. It had first flown at Woodley in May 1936—but only fifty of them were ever manufactured, and a number of them were operated by the Thanet Aero Club.

RAF Manston was well-represented at the opening of the airport. An Avro Anson, a Hawker Hind, and the Westland Wallace from the Practice Flight

The scene at Ramsgate Airport's official opening, on 3 July 1937. (*Margate Museum*)

flew the short distance to Ramsgate to join the various types of aircraft on display there. In the official guest-list there is no mention of Group Captain Strugnell attending the opening, but Wg Cdr Bryson and Wg Cdr Langford Sainsbury were there with their wives. Flight Lieutenants W. E. Knowlden and C. E. Eckersley Maslin also attended the luncheon, along with Flying Officers F. E. M. Cooper, S. Mouatt, and Pilot Officer P. D. P. Conmore. While those present took tea, the RAF Band played on the lawn in front of the club house (a part of the administrative building).

Recently-promoted Squadron Leader Charles Edward Eckersley Maslin had been appointed as the airport manager, and was also the chief pilot and instructor there. Eckersley Maslin was an extremely interesting character who had joined the Argyle and Sutherland when underage by giving a false date of birth. It was only after he was wounded in France (where he was shot in the face and lost most of his front teeth) that it was discovered he was only sixteen years old. He was sent back to Bedford School after recovering.

After coming of age Eckersley Maslin attempted to join the army and the Royal Navy, but he failed the medicals because of his flat feet and lack of teeth; as an alternative, he studied medicine for a year. Yearning for more excitement, Eckersley Maslin went to Ireland and joined the Royal Irish Constabulary, where on two occasions he was badly injured by bomb blast. In 1922, when the RIC was disbanded, he went to South Africa and joined the South African Mounted Police. He took up sparring there, but ended up being knocked out while boxing the South-African champion. If that was not enough, following his recovery he was weakened by two bouts of Blackwater Fever. He had to leave the force as a result of his illness and medical conditions.

In 1925 Eckersley Maslin joined the RAF on a short service commission while in Egypt; following his flying training, he was posted to No. 28 Squadron in India. While he was in Karachi he was appointed as the test pilot for the RAF aircraft which had been flown in. One airman who worked under him was AC Shaw (T. E. Lawrence). While at Karachi he also got to know a number of well-known aviators—including Jim and Amy Mollison, with whom he became good friends.

Eckersley Maslin had been confirmed in the rank of Pilot Officer in January 1926. His promotion to the rank of Flight Lieutenant followed in 1931, but shortly afterwards he transferred to the RAF Reserve and travelled home to become a civil pilot. Initially he worked at Shanklin, on the Isle of Wight, before moving to Portsmouth, where he became superintendent of the airport. He later moved to Jersey Airways, where he got to know Whitney Straight—who then appointed him as manager of Ramsgate Airport. Eckersley Maslin never served at Manston, but he was a very popular figure at Ramsgate Airport.

There was a flying display after the speeches on the airport's opening day, with performances from a Tipsy Monoplane and a Short Scion Senior—ably demonstrated by its pilot, Mr H. J. Piper. The Lockheed 12 Junior Electra (in which Lord Beaverbrook had flown down) was also demonstrated by its regular pilot, Mr Downes. At the end of the afternoon guests were taken on pleasure flights around the island in the D. H. Dragon, the Short Scion, and Thanet Aero Club's Hornet Moth.

Ramsgate Airport also facilitated Ramsgate Flying Centre, which was, in effect, a holiday camp where visitors and families could stay for a number of weeks. Just after the airport had opened, an article was published in a magazine by a Mrs E. W. Goodwin, who had stayed at the centre with her husband and child. She described how they had left Victoria Station by train and were met at Broadstairs Station by an airport car. They were then driven to the airport, where they were accommodated in a tent that had a wooden floor. They dined in the airport's restaurant, and taken by an airport car to Ramsgate, where they saw the film *Lost Horizon*. Mrs Goodwin recollected that they dined on excellent food and were well looked-after over the two weeks; she wrote that she would definitely recommend the Flying Centre Holiday to her friends.

Just over two weeks after the airport had officially opened, No. 611 'West Lancashire' Squadron arrived to hold its summer camp from 17–31 July. The squadron, equipped with the Hawker Hart as a day-bomber unit, had been formed at Hendon in February 1936. In May of that year, its base moved to Speke airport. Such units would traditionally have held their camps at RAF Manston, but the sheer number of service personnel posted there and the expansion of No. 3 SoTT meant that there was no space to accommodate them.

Ramsgate Airport provided all the facilities that the squadron required, and was close to the town for recreational purposes. RAF Manston was also just a short ride up the road. No. 611 Squadron was the first of several RAF units to hold its summer camps at Ramsgate Airport; soon a number of other auxiliary units arrived, and they were accommodated in bell tents by the side of the airfield.

One other auxiliary unit to hold its summer camp at Ramsgate Airport was No. 609 'West Riding' Squadron, which was based at Yeadon Airport (situated between Leeds and Bradford). It had been formed as a day-bomber unit in February 1936, and was equipped with the Hawker Hart and Avro Tutor for training purposes. The unit took nine aircraft to Ramsgate, and some of the airmen were lucky enough to be flown down in a Boulton & Paul Overstrand. Amongst the auxiliary airmen who attended the camp were Corporal Daniels, Jack Lister, L. Garrit, and P. Kendall. Members of the squadron really enjoyed being in Thanet. During their off-duty time, they went swimming at the beach on Broadstairs and took a boat trip from Margate on the Queen of Thanet.

A number of airmen took their first flight during the summer camp—including Jack Lister, who went flying in a Hawker Hart with Plt Off.

Drummond-Hay. As he was being fitted with the harness and parachute, he became aware that there was no seat for him and he would have to stand behind the pilot. This made him fearful of dropping out of the aircraft if the pilot looped the loop, but he then discovered that there was an anchor point at the bottom of the cockpit and a strap that fitted to his harness. He thoroughly enjoyed his flight around the coast of Thanet, and the sight of people waving on the beaches gave him a real thrill. It was an experience that he remembered for the rest of his life.

Former Capt. Bertie Arthur Millson DFC, instructor at the School of Air Navigation, died on 15 August. He was buried in Minster Cemetery a few days later. Throughout the year or so that he had been instructing at Manston he had gained the respect of his fellow officers and airmen, and there were many fine tributes to him during his funeral. Wg Cdr Bryson, the Officer Commanding No. 3 SOTT, and Sqn Ldr Wright, the station Adjutant, were the senior officers who represented RAF Manston.

Capt. Millson's coffin was carried to Minster on an RAF tender, accompanied by the sombre strains of Chopin's Funeral March as played by the station band. The station's chaplain, the Reverend M. H. Edwards, met the burial party at the cemetery gates before carrying out the committal service. As the last rites were performed, a firing party of forty airmen fired a volley into the air. As a final tribute, all the officers and airmen slowly filed past Captain Millson's grave—where many wreaths and flowers had been laid.

The Thanet Air Day took place on Saturday 21 August. There was free admission for the general public, with an advert in the local press promising flying aerobatics at 300 mph, a parachute leap, demonstration flying, and pleasure flights; however, the main attraction was the Thanet Air Race. There had been twenty-one entries in the air race, but only sixteen competitors took part. Amongst them was Mr Alex Henshaw, who was flying a Mew Gull. Geoffrey de Havilland was another entrant, flying an aeroplane known as the D.H. TK2, which had been designed by students at de Havilland's Aeronautical Technical School. It had already competed in a number of air races, and had taken second place in the Heston–Newcastle Race in early July.

In addition to the entries from well-known British companies, the Thanet Air Race also attracted three entries from Germany. Two of these were from companies that would soon strike terror into the hearts of people in Thanet: Messerschmitt and Focke-Wulf. The other German entry was a Klemm; all three were representatives of the Aero Club Von Deutschland. The fourth foreign entry was a low-wing monoplane from Latvia, flown by Jaris Vitol.

The weather was not good on the morning of the 21st, with strong winds threatening to disrupt the event—but this did not stop a huge number of people from attending. At the opening of the event Alderman H. Stead, the Mayor of Ramsgate, said that he could visualise a day when the airport would be twice the size, and aeroplanes from all over the world would land there. Mr Whitney Straight said that Ramsgate was proud of its new airport, and that it would continue to be a success—pointing out that the Thanet Air Race was now an annual event.

The course for the race was 25 miles long and made up of three laps, with the turning points being the chimney of the economic laundry, Richborough, and Reculver Towers. The handicappers were Capt. Dancy and Mr Rowarth. The first prize was £50 cash and the Vye Trophy, while the second prize was £25 cash and a replica trophy—the third prize was £10. While Mr Barnes kept the crowd informed on what was going on in the race over the loudspeakers, in the meantime there were demonstrations of parachuting and gliding. There were murmurs from the crowd when it was announced that one of the three women to fly in the race, Miss Gladys Bachelor, had been disqualified for failing to turn at the correct point.

Taking the handicaps into account, the winner of the race was a Taylor Cub flown by Mr P. B. Elewell from London, with a speed of 71 mph and a time of fifty-five minutes and forty-three seconds. Second place was awarded to the Spartan Arrow flown by Flt Lt H. J. A. Edwards, who had a speed of 92 mph and a flying time of forty-three minutes and fifteen seconds. In third place was future Spitfire test pilot Alex Henshaw, with a fantastic speed of 207 mph and a flying time of just nineteen minutes and seventeen seconds. An Avro 504 flown by Capt. Philips was fourth, and the Latvian monoplane flown by Mr. J Vitols was fifth. Had Miss Bachelor not been disqualified she would have finished third. Miss Mabel Glass, flying a Gipsy Moth, completed the course and finished ninth.

Flt Lt H. J. A. Edwards, who was stationed at Manston, was an experienced racing pilot who had flown in the King's Cup Races in 1932, 1934, and 1935. He held an 'A' and 'B' licence, a second-class Navigator's Certificate, and 2,050 hours in his log book. In 1935 he had finished second.

The first fatal incident at Ramsgate Airport occurred on Tuesday 24 August, just a few days after the Thanet Air Day. Mr David Holliday Jorge, described as a holiday relief pilot, was in the aircraft that crashed to the ground. The aircraft was G-AEEN, a British Aircraft Corporation Drone, described as an ultra-light type and powered by a 600 cc Douglas motorcycle engine. For most of the day Mr Jorge had been taking tourists on flights around Thanet. However, the stream of potential passengers dried up at around 6 p.m., and it was reported that he seemed bored by the lack of action. He borrowed an aircraft which belonged to Mr Albert Bachelor, but was being flown by Mr W. M. C. Peatfield (a member of the Thanet Aero Club).

The incident was reported in the *East Kent Times* the next day, with the headline: 'Dive to Death: Pilot Killed at Ramsgate Air Port. Fatal Boredom'. It claimed that Mr Jorge's last flight was one which could be described by the phrase 'the truth is stranger than fiction. After taking off Mr Jorge flew back towards the airfield, possibly because a party of tourists had arrived who wanted to go up on a pleasure flight, and he had seen them from the air. He was turning back into the wind, at a height of approximately 100 feet, when the aircraft suddenly went into a spin. The plane plunged to earth, with the engine running on full power.

It crashed almost exactly in the middle of the airfield. It was reported that the aircraft had hit the ground with such force that the engine was torn from its mountings, and had ended up some distance from rest of the wreckage. Emergency vehicles were called to the scene, including a fire engine and an ambulance. Amongst those first to arrive were the crew of an ambulance belonging to No. 608 'North Riding' Squadron of the AAF, which was holding its summer camp at Ramsgate Airport between 15–29 August.

No. 608 Squadron was based at RAF Thornaby, near York, and had its own band to entertain the crowds. It was equipped with the Hawker Demon. At time of the crash several of their planes were in the air and due to land, so arrangements had to be made for them to touch down safely, away from the burning wreckage. A car travelled in front of the RAF ambulance in order to clear the traffic, but Mr Jorge was already dead by the time he reached Ramsgate General Hospital. This was an unfortunate incident, and the general opinion was that if Mr Jorge had been little more patient then he would not have lost his life.

10

Changing Times

Despite the fact that No. 3 School of Technical Training had drastically grown in numbers, well beyond the original expectations, in there was a reduction in the number of administrative squadrons in September 1937. They were reduced from four to two, leaving just 'B' and 'C' Squadrons.

A number of additional buildings were erected on the airfield in early September. Amongst these were three portable steel hangars which were put up on the north-west side, close to the Reception Flight. At about the same time, a smoke wind indicator was installed on the airfield so that pilots could read wind strength and direction more easily.

October was a busy month for the school, and on the 27th the RAF's Inspector General Sir Edward Ellington paid a visit and inspected the workshops. Sir Edward had been appointed to the post in September, and was approaching the end of an illustrious service career; he had served twice as the principal Aide-de-Camp to the King, and as Chief of Air Staff in May 1933. There were also changes to the command of No. 3 SoTT in October, when Wing Commander Ernest John Dennis Townsend took over from Wg Cdr Bryson GC MC DFC. It is not clear from the records what happened to Wg Cdr Bryson when he left Manston, but in November 1938 he was promoted to the rank of Group Captain; he remained in the RAF until 1943.

Townsend was a Canadian who had studied at the Gentlemen's Royal Military College Kingston before travelling to Britain, where he had joined the Royal Field Artillery in January 1915. In early 1916 he re-mustered to the Royal Flying Corps as an observer, but he later trained as a pilot; he was subsequently posted to No. 60 Squadron in 1917. In the early 1920s Townsend studied at Cambridge and London Universities, before being posted to the aircraft depot in Iraq as a Staff Officer. He later served as the senior engineering officer at both Upper Heyford and HQ Western Area, before serving for a second time in Iraq. He was posted to Manston from there.

On 8 October 1937 Lieutenant-Commander Spencer Grey DSO died after falling off the roof of his home in London, while trying to rig up an aerial. He had been the first airman to land on the Isle of Thanet, in April 1912. To have died under such circumstances was a tragic end for an officer who had achieved so much, and carried out some of the first and most daring raids of the First World War.

There was an event held on 20 October which would normally have been quite unpopular amongst those in the ranks—a physical training exercise, involving a large number of airmen. It was noted that the mass PT exercise had proved quite successful, partly due to the aid of a loudspeaker. An optimistic note in the ORB claimed that exercise had encouraged renewed interest in PT in all those taking part.

November was in interesting month for the pupils and staff of No. 3 SoTT. Eight showcases of exercises carried out by pupils were submitted to the HQ of RAF Recruiting at Victory House. The showcases involved samples of exercises and work carried out by metal workers, and it was to be used for propaganda purposes. A report from the air ministry was quite positive, confirming that the showcases had been useful and had created general interest for the purposes of recruitment.

On 17 November, Squadron Leader G. T. H. Pack, the officer commanding training, visited the Vickers Works in Weybridge with education officer Mr. R. J. Steeple Esquire. The purpose of their visit was to obtain the latest data on the construction of geodetic aircraft, such as the Wellington. Vickers were at the forefront of geodetic design, which had first been used in the Wellesley (first flown in June 1935).

The following day Sqn Ldr Pack, along with forty other servicemen and civilian instructors, visited the Ford plant at Dagenham. The purpose of that visit was to obtain information about the processes of vehicle manufacture. In addition to this, on 24 November a lecture was given at Manston by a representative from de Havilland, who spoke about variable pitch airscrews (propellers).

Following the addition of the three steel portable hangars erected in September, a second Bessonneau Hangar was put up next to the one that had been built in March. This was again erected on the north-west side of the airfield.

By the end of December 1937 several hundred more regular and reserve officers had successfully taken the parachute course examinations.

	Examined	Passed
'A' Officers		
Parachute	348	348
Reserve Officers	7	7
'B' Airmen		
Parachute	212	212
Naval R.	33	33
Driver Petrol	363	343
Fabric Worker	136	133
Fitter A.E.	644	601
Metal Rigger	323	294
Mates	3,598	3,463
A.A.F. & S.R.	47	47
Class 'E' Reserve	35	35
Aircraft Welding (*Airmen*)	27	27
Aircraft Welding (*Naval R.*)	23	23
Aero Engines (*Naval R.*)	7	7

A total of 5,570 trainees had been examined in 1937, with 5,386 passing; this gave No. 3 SoTT a 96 per cent pass rate.

Despite the diversity of the courses, and the school's high pass rate, at the beginning of January 1938 there were the first signs that No. 3 SoTT might be moved away from RAF Manston. A note in the school's ORB stated that 'tentative instructions were received about the opening of Number 3 School of Technical Training at St Athan, Wales'. There was no mention of whether St Athan would simply absorb the overspill from Manston, or whether it would completely take over responsibility for the school.

A short while later it was confirmed that some sections of the SoTT would be established at St Athan, which would be known as No. 4 SoTT. It was suggested that the move would just be a temporary measure, but it would involve a significant number of pupils and staff being absorbed from Manston. There was no mention of the future of the unit at Manston, but reading between the lines suggests that it was planned to be closed down.

January was a busy month for the Commanding Officer of the school, Wg Cdr Townsend, who was appointed as OC sports officer and—in the event of enemy attack—the gas officer. He and Sqn Ldr Pack attended conference at the RAF records office, in Ruislip, concerning the trade testing of airmen. A few days later he visited HQ No. 24 Group at Halton, where he attended a

A view of the Prospect Inn at Minster, in Ramsgate. This is an image of one of its two 'funnels', taken through a window that was fashioned as a porthole to emphasise its maritime theme. The Prospect opened in 1938, and was one of two local pubs frequented by the airmen at Manston; the other was the Jolly Farmer, in Manston Village. The Prospect Inn is now a Holiday Inn Express. (*Author's collection*)

lecture on aircraft design in stressed-skin construction.

On 1 February the wing commander visited the police college at Hendon, in order to see how it trained police drivers. He was accompanied by Sqn Ldr Pack and Flying Officer Mather. The authorities were taking the potential threat of gas warfare very seriously, and so on 7th Sqn Ldr Pack was briefly attached to the depot at Uxbridge so he could attend a ten-day course on anti-gas measures. Visits to industrial sites were becoming a regular occurrence, and on the 10th a number of non-commissioned officers from technical trades made visits to the Rolls Royce factory in Derby and Fairey's works in Bristol. They also visited the Vickers factory at Weybridge again, and the Hawker Engineering Works in Kingston.

At the beginning of April there was further correspondence from the Air Ministry about the future of No. 3 SoTT. The memorandum, dated 18 February, stated that the intention was for the school to move to Weston-Super-Mare after 1940. Meanwhile, to relieve the problem of the overcrowded accommodation at Manston, it was arranged that 500 Mates 'Fitters III' would be trained at Cardington in September 1938. There was no mention of St Athan, or about the forming of No. 4 School.

In February 1938 the Prospect Inn public house opened. It was situated at the top of Tothill Street, in Minster, on the south-west side of the airfield, and it was a popular venue for airmen and officers serving at RAF Manston. The only other public house in the vicinity of the airfield was the Jolly Farmer, in Manston village, but the Prospect was on the main Ramsgate to Canterbury London road—whereas the Jolly Farmer was hidden away.

The first landlord and landlady of the Prospect Inn were Mr and Mrs Algy Aldridge. They had previously managed the Captain Digby at Kingsdown, and when they moved to the Prospect Inn the Captain Digby was taken over by the co-author's (John William's) grandfather. The Prospect Inn belonged to the brewery run by Thompson and Wotton—one of Britain's oldest brewers, which can trace its history back to 1680. The inn remained a firm favourite for the airmen and officers serving at RAF Manston until it was closed down in the mid-1970s. Perhaps due to the Prospect's links to the station, rumours were often spread that it was haunted. Claims used to circulate that people staying at the pub over the years had been awoken in the early hours by ghoulish airmen, throwing stones at the windows to get their attention.

The Prospect Inn had been built in the art-deco style of the 1930s, but what was special about its design was that it depicted an ocean liner. The architect was Oliver Hill, and the official style of the building was referred to as 'international modern Cunard'. With a curved frontage to represent the bridge, and two small funnels on each side, from certain angles it clearly resembles a ship—but it is not known which one it was based on. There are rumours that its design was influenced by the *Queen Mary*, which was launched in 1935, but that cannot be confirmed. Hill had been involved with the design of a number of other stylish buildings, including Clivedon Palace in London and The Midland Hotel in Morecombe. However, the Prospect Inn was the only public house he designed.

There were royal visitors at RAF Manston on Thursday 12 May 1938, when His Royal Highness the Duke of Kent arrived after opening some new buildings at King's School in Canterbury. He drove himself from Canterbury to Manston, accompanied by escort police cars which were commanded by Superintendent Wheatley of the St Augustine's in Kent County Constabulary. After arriving at the station he was met by the station's commander, Group Captain Strugnell, and Flt Lt Chadwick, who was acting as the Adjutant. It was only a brief visit, and after exchanging the usual pleasantries His Royal Highness boarded his private plane and flew off. It was noted in the *East Kent Times* that very few people noticed either his arrival or his departure.

On 14 May 1938 the strength of No. 3 SoTT totalled ten officers, eight education officers, and a permanent staff of 193 officers and NCOs. There were also seventy-three civilians serving on the staff, and the total number of personnel was 2,511.

11

A State of Emergency

On 21 May, a brief detachment was sent from No. 3 SoTT to Ypres, in France. It was made up of one officer, eight flight sergeants, four corporals, and thirty-eight airmen. The occasion was the unveiling of a memorial in Ypres Cathedral, which was dedicated to the British Army, the RAF, and the memory of the late King Albert of the Belgians. The service had been organised by the Ypres League, and amongst those present were King Leopold of Belgium and the Bishop of Bruges, who led the service. It was held in Saint Martin's Cathedral, which had been rebuilt to its original style and design after being completely destroyed by the end of the First World War.

Part of the memorial in the cathedral was a rose window—said to be the largest in Belgium—and a smaller window, in which appeared the crests of Belgium, the RAF, and the 5th Royal Inniskilling Dragoon Guards. An inscription on a tablet read:

> To the Glory of God and in Honoured Memory of Albert I, King of Belgians, Knight of the Garter, Field Marshal of the British Army and Colonel in Chief of the 5th Royal Inniskilling Dragoon Guards, the Rose Window in the south Transept is given to Belgium by the British Army and Royal Air Force.

Empire Air Day was observed at RAF Manston on 28 May. The workshops of No. 3 SoTT were thrown open to the public, and an arts and crafts exhibition was held. Air raid precautions were a popular topic, and one of the displays was organised to show the horrors of modern warfare. A headline in the local paper read: 'Cameos of War. Vivid Demonstration by RAF Manston. Empire Air Day Thrills'. This was in reference to the scene that was played out at the base, involving the detonations of gun cotton, well-placed smoke candles, and simulated casualties. These were all used to represent the realities of an air raid, especially ones where bombs containing gas were dropped.

Everyone in Thanet was used to the sight of the lightly-armed Avro Ansons of No. 48 Squadron gyrating around the sky. According to the press, however, the public was still terrified by the sight of the Ansons diving towards the ground with their engines flat out, being chased by a hoard of Hawker Hind fighters from No. 500 Squadron. A makeshift building was erected on the edge of the flying area to represent a house or group of buildings that were being attacked from the air. Three specially-camouflaged Ansons acted as the attacking force—they took off and disappeared from view, before returning and diving towards their target.

The poor visibility added to rather than distracted from the effectiveness of the mock attack, as the Hawker Hinds rose into the air to intercept the Ansons. According to the newspaper, there was minute after minute of breath-taking thrills. The Hinds repeatedly dived into the arrowhead of the Anson's formation in an attempt to break it up, and for a while it seemed as though a collision was inevitable—however, at the last moment the Anson or Hind always broke away.

The makeshift building received a hit. Turf and pieces of wood flew off in all directions, as grey smoke filled the air and fire erupted from every opening. Gas-warning sirens howled and fire alarms rang out as fire engines, ambulances, and lorries (acting as gas-decontamination squads) raced to the scene. By the end of the action it appeared as if one of the Ansons had been shot down, and the crowd was excited when they saw the crew 'abandoning' their aircraft. All those taking part in the ground were in their fighting kit, and according to newspaper reports the mock attack was about as realistic as it could have been.

A female reporter from the *East Kent Times* was allowed on board one of the Ansons and wrote about her experience, under the headline: 'Power diving and what it feels like. (By Our Lady Reporter)'. The reporter, who remained anonymous, wrote that she had experienced her very first flight on Saturday in one of the set pieces during Empire Air Day. She wrote, 'Power dives of about 1,500 feet, at a hundred or two hundred miles per hour, are all very well for people who make flying a daily habit, but for a person who is up for the first time...' At one point she described how she had felt that she was falling into space, and had attempted to grab a strut to save herself—only to realise that the strut was falling too. This made her feel quite uncanny.

Someone later asked her if her insides followed on when the aircraft had flattened out after the dive, but she said she could not remember because of the overriding fear that the pilot might do it all over again. She shouted out to the pilot to ask how high they were, and he replied '25 feet'—but she was convinced that he had got it wrong, and that they were so low that he must have meant 25 inches. Perhaps there was just a hint of exaggeration, and maybe it had not been a good idea for the reporter to experience her first flight on such an occasion.

There was a second set piece after the mock attack, involving nine of No. 48 Squadron's Ansons 'bombing' a convoy of lorries. There was also action involving other types of aircraft—for instance, there was a brilliant display of aerobatics by three Gloster Gauntlets from Biggin Hill. The Gauntlet had first flown in 1933, and entered service with the RAF when No. 19 Squadron was re-equipped with it in 1935. The three Gauntlets in the display were so perfect that it gave the illusion that they were tied together, encouraging gasps of admiration from their fellow airmen who were watching on the ground. No. 500 Squadron, the resident reserve unit at Manston, also gained a lot of applause for its part in making Empire Air Day a magnificent occasion, and were described in the press as the 'terriers' of the air force.

For the more daring members of the public, there was an opportunity to experience passing through a gas chamber and to test a new type of gas mask; the prospect of a gas attack was terrifying. Empire Air Day happened to coincide with the visit of the three Swedish experts on civilian warfare to Manston; they arrived in Ramsgate on Monday 23 May, and were greeted by Mr A. E. Hill, the South Eastern Regional Air Raid Precautions Inspector. They then met the Mayor of Ramsgate, Alderman W. T. Smith, and Chairman of the ARP Committee, Councillor Huddlestone, before going on to inspect the town's ARP activities.

The Swedish representatives were first shown the organisation on paper, but they soon had a demonstration about the practical side of things. They were shown around the stores, the designated gas-protected room, the decontamination room, and the appliances. Later, at Ramsgate fire station, Chief Officer F. C. West explained the use of auxiliary fire-fighting equipment before giving a demonstration on how to deal with an incendiary bomb. At the end of the day the Swedish delegation said they were greatly impressed with what they had seen in Ramsgate, comparing it favourably to similar organisations they had inspected in France and other parts of Europe.

On Saturday 4 June, another lady had an exciting time during her first flight when the dual-control Miles Magister in which she was flying suffered an engine failure. The Magister was a single-engine aircraft, used exclusively to train RAF pilots. The cockpit was in a tandem configuration, with the instructor flying it from the rear seat.

The incident occurred while the aircraft was being flown by Mr John Dade, an instructor at Ramsgate Airport who was engaged in training members of the Women's Auxiliary Air Force. His pupil—Miss Betty Wase, of Beckenham— must have wondered what was happening when the engine stopped and the aircraft flew across the flight path of a D. H. Dragon, flown by Squadron Leader Eckersley Maslin. Eckersley Maslin later told the press that he saw the Magister flying above him, at around 1,500 feet, when it suddenly dived across his bows—He realised that the pilot was in some difficulty. He followed the Magister down, descending and circling in figures of eight until it reached the ground. It had no more than 80 yards to run before it would have gone over the edge of a cliff.

As Eckersley Maslin watched Mr Dade struggle with the controls, he observed that the only field in which he could make a safe landing was on the edge of the cliffs, and also contained a number of cows and horses which were out grazing. There were a number of posts that Mr Dade had to avoid as he approached the ground, and he had to use the rudder to side slip, gently moving the tail from side to side. Eckersley Maslin saw the aircraft straighten out and make a perfect three-point landing behind the Coast Guard cottages, close to Little Cliffs End Farm. The Magister came to rest no more than 20 feet from the fence that guarded the end of the cliff—and the 100-foot drop to the rocks and sea below.

Mr Dade was not affected by what had happened, and was later reported to say, 'It's all in a day's work. The engine just cut out, and all I did was to land the bus.' The female passenger, Miss Wade, said she was more interested than frightened, and that at first she had thought that the engine cutting out was part of her flying lesson—it was not until they landed that she realised how close to death she had been. Eckersley Maslin said that it was nothing more than a miracle for Mr Dade to have landed safely under such circumstances.

Captain H. H. Balfour, local MP and the Under Secretary of State for Air, visited RAF Manston on 18 June in order to tour the workshops of No. 3 SoTT and inspect the airmen's accommodation. He arrived by air at approximately 1 p.m., and after the usual protocol of meeting the station's Commander Officer, Group Captain Strugnell, he carried out his inspection. He then took lunch in the officers' mess before leaving again, by air, to carry out inspections at a number of other RAF stations. However, it was reported that he had expressed satisfaction with what he had seen before departing.

No. 3 SoTT was called upon again on the 27th to provide a detachment to Canterbury, where a service for seamen took place and a red ensign was deposited in the cathedral. One officer and 100 airmen took part in the service and subsequent ceremonial parade, under the command of Sqn Ldr Pack.

There was something of a setback for the development of Ramsgate Municipal Airport that June. The general purposes committee of Broadstairs and St Peter's urban district council informed the Ministry of Health that it was not prepared to reserve land in the town planning scheme for the expansion of the airport. It was also unwilling to agree to the imposition of height restrictions on properties which might be built upon the adjoining land. The airport had fallen foul of the fact that it was located closer to Broadstairs and St Peters than Ramsgate, and those boroughs had always opposed the development of the airport.

Despite this setback, a new air service was inaugurated on Tuesday 26 July between Thanet and London. The first flight into Ramsgate carried a party of town councillors from Romford, where the London airfield was situated. Amongst them was the Mayoress, Mrs Allen, who was accompanied by her daughter. They were met by the Mayor of Ramsgate, Alderman W. T. Smith, who was waiting at Ramsgate to take the return flight to Romford with a group of other town councillors. Amongst them was the Mayor of Margate, Councillor G. B. Farrar, and—although his council had opposed the expansion scheme—Councillor F. Foster, the chairman of Broadstairs and St Peter's urban district council, was also present.

The aircraft was a D.H. 84 de Havilland Dragon, flown by Sqn Ldr Eckersley Maslin, with the inaugural service operated by Southern Airways. Mr Whitney Straight had flown down to Ramsgate just ahead of the Dragon, accompanied by one of the directors of the company, Mr Gordon. Southern Airways was a subsidiary of the Straight Corporation, as was Western Airways, and the corporation had obtained exclusive rights to operate from Romford Airport. Building work at Romford Airport had not yet been completed, but at this time it was said to be the nearest airport to the centre of London.

Another tragic incident occurred on 17 July, causing two fatalities. A Miles Whitney Straight, G-AFEU, which belonged to the Thanet Aero Club crashed into the sea off the coast of Cliftonville. The Aircraft was being flown by nineteen-year-old Edmund Leonard George Betts, with sixteen-year-old Marjorie Walker as his passenger. Mr Betts was buried in Margate's St John Cemetery, and his grave is marked by a headstone of rough-hewn granite, appropriately topped by a small aeroplane sculpted from white marble. This was not the first fatal incident involving this type of plane, but the aircraft was generally well-received in spite of this. Twenty-three Miles Witney Straights would later be pressed into service with the military.

At the beginning of August the Air Ministry sent what were described in the ORB as 'tentative instructions' for a new syllabus of training at No. 3 SoTT. The letter, *799640/38/Tech.d/d 3.8.38,* introduced the new training regime for aircraft hands mechanics and flight-riggers. It stipulated that the trade of mate would cease as soon as the present courses were completed.

On 1 September No. 48 Squadron moved from Manston to RAF Eastchurch, on the Isle of Sheppey. The unit, which at one point had eighty Avro Ansons on its strength, had handed over its training role to the School of Air Navigation.

The Munich Crisis occurred in September 1938, during which Hitler planned to occupy the parts of Czechoslovakia known as the Sudetenland. The crisis had a severe effect on the activities of most RAF stations, and on 25 September the ORB noted that they were in a state of emergency, during which all leave would be cancelled. All normal training at No. 3 SoTT was suspended, with the situation growing so serious that many of the airmen were made to dig trenches on the station. Bombs and ammunition were removed from stores, and all service personnel and civilians were issued with gas masks.

In November there were further changes to the titles of some courses at No. 3 SoTT, after it had received Air Ministry order 'A' 442/38. The existing courses for training metal riggers and fitters (aero-engine) were to be re-designated as 'Fitter 1' (airframe) and 'Fitter II' (engine).

After losing No. 48 Squadron at the beginning of September, on the 28th No. 500 Squadron also left the station for RAF Detling. The unit had formed at Manston in March 1931, and left behind many happy memories of their seven years in Thanet. The change came about because the unit was about to be transferred to central command; within a few months it would be re-equipped with the Avro Anson. Detling is approximately 35 miles from Manston, and so some form of transport must have been arranged for the airmen who lived in Thanet.

The winter of 1938 was particularly harsh, and the severely cold weather seriously affected the training program—the temperature in the workshops plummeted towards freezing, as snow and strong cold winds added to the problem. A number of oil stoves were requisitioned from the stores depot at Kidbrooke in an attempt to make things warmer, but they only raised the temperature a few degrees; enough to make it bearable. The bad weather continued until the end of December, when the school shut down and everyone went on Christmas leave.

	Examined	Passed
'A' Officers		
Officers Parachute Courses	323	322
Officers Reserve Courses	11	11
Warrant Shiprights R.N.		
Aircraft Maintenance Course	4	4
'B' Airmen		
Fabric Workers	101	98
Parachute Course	197	194
Metal Rigger	350	334
Metal Worker	70	70
Fitter AE	311	308
FM/FR	739	739
Driver Petrol	428	421
Mates	4,501	4,155

Auxiliary Air Force

Fitter AE	22	22
Metal Rigger	11	11
Fabric Worker	1	1
Reservist		
Fitter AE	5	5
Carpenter	2	2
Fabric Worker	7	7
Rigger Aero	2	2
Fitter DF	1	1
ACH	1	1
Naval Ratings		
Parachute Course	27	27
Aircraft Welding Course	10	9
Aero Engine Course	6	5
Total	**5,792**	**5,424**

Total Movements 1938

Airmen Personnel	In	Out	Total
Postings	6,736	6,591	13,327
Attachments	311	325	636
Total	**7,047**	**6,916**	**13,963**

Number 1 Section OC Flying Officer A. Marks
Number 2 Section OC Flying Officer A. L. Cockburn
Number 3 Section OC Flying Officer C. L. Trevithick

Officers at the school included CO Wing Commander Townsend and the Chief Training Officer Sqn Ldr C. H. V. Hayman, who had seemingly replaced Sqn Ldr Pack. The Adjutant was Flight Lieutenant A. J. P. Groom, who was serving in the RAF Reserve. The civilian assistant Adjutant was the long-serving former Flight Lieutenant C. Fenn, and the civilian engineering assistant was J. N. Eastcott

Officers at the school included CO Wing Commander Townsend and the chief training officer, Sqn Ldr C. H. V. Hayman, who had seemingly replaced Sqn Ldr Pack. The Adjutant was Flight Lieutenant A. J. P. Groom who was serving in the RAF Reserve. The civilian assistant Adjutant was the long serving former Flt Lt C. Fenn, and the civilian engineering assistant J. N. Eastcott (later RAF).

12

An Eventful Year

In the first week of January, a meeting of the Air Raid Preparation Committee of Ramsgate town council made a decision that would end up saving hundreds—if not thousands—of lives. This decision, reached unanimously, was to press forward with a tunnel-shelter scheme. The idea that the people of Ramsgate could use tunnels to shelter from hostile air attacks had been proposed the previous May; the town already had a small network of underground tunnels, which had previously been used to house an underground electric railway. It was planned that these would form the basis for a wider system of tunnels and galleries.

When the scheme of tunnels had first been presented to the Home Office it did not receive immediate approval—the town was told that it would not receive permission to establish them, despite it being a good idea, as the estimated cost was initially around £80,000. However, Ramsgate ARPC was determined to go ahead with the scheme, and a later study suggested that the work could be completed over four months at the cost of no more than £50,000.

Perhaps due to the pressures of the time, it seems that the *East Kent Times* was not allowed to publish anything more interesting on military affairs than the 'Manston RAF Sports News'. The main part of this report, written by someone identified as 'Ace', concerned a football match between Bobby's Football and Athletic Club and the School of Air Navigation. Despite the school's team being better on paper, they were beaten 5–2 in conditions that were described as a mud bath.

There was also a mention of Manston's first 11 football team, who had reached the third round of the RAF Senior Cup and were unbeaten in the league. The *East Kent Times* reported that RAF Manston now organised inter-section games and gave those who were training on short courses the chance to prove themselves. A number of players from the first eleven had recently been posted out, and Fg Off. Acquaroff (a former RAF team player) was helping to organise it again.

The Director of Training and Air Officer Commanding No. 24 Group, Air Cdre Paul Copeland Maltby, visited Manston and toured the workshops of No. 3 SoTT on 14 February—responding to reports of the need for extra accommodation, as well as discussing other matters relating to training. Air Cdre Maltby had been appointed to the post in 1938, after serving as AOC of the RAF in the Mediterranean. The school was attracting quite a number of important visitors, with two members of the establishment committee from the Air Ministry arriving to inspect the unit two days later.

Doctor Hermann Görtz—the so-called Manston Spy—was released from Maidstone Prison on Saturday 25 February after serving three years of the four-year sentence that he had received in March 1936. Officers from Scotland Yard escorted Görtz to Grimsby, where he boarded a ship bound for Hamburg. The now forty-seven-year-old Görtz had made a number of interesting Irish connections while he had been in prison, ensuring that this would not be the last time the security services would hear of him.

In March the Inspector General of the RAF Sir Edward Ellington inspected the pupils undergoing training. Air Cdre Maltby also visited the unit again, and a gas alarm took place to inspect all anti-gas measures. Other defences coming under scrutiny included the dug-outs (which remained from the First World War) and trenches which had been dug and covered in more recently. It is not known where exactly the dug-outs were located, but it is strange that they were still in use—it had previously been mentioned in the ORB that these defensive positions had collapsed after the timbers that supported them had been removed.

At the beginning of April 125 airmen arrived at the school, the first students for the new trade of Fitters II (A). At the same time, it was announced that Wg Cr Townsend had been promoted to Group Captain. Wg Cdr Seymour Stewart Benson AFC took over the command of No. 3 SoTT on 5 May. He had been awarded a permanent commission in 1919, later studying at Cambridge University. In 1932 he had been seconded to the Japanese Navy, but afterwards spent a considerable amount of time serving as an engineering officer in Iraq. Wg Cdr Townsend was posted out to HQ No. 41 Group, and Wg Cdr Benson would spend very little time at the school before he was also posted to another unit.

Another sign that the war was imminent was the growing recruitment campaign, carried out by a number of non-commissioned officers and airmen from RAF Manston and the SoTT. This campaign took place in the local towns of Ramsgate, Margate, and Broadstairs, but also in the Medway town of Faversham.

On 27 May 1939, No. 3 SoTT received the news that the design and artwork for its crest and badge had been approved by His Majesty the King. The badge was presented to the unit during a formal parade, attended by

Air Cdre Maltby. It had taken nearly eight years for the badge to get royal approval, after being initially approved by the Air Ministry on 12 June 1931 (in a letter referenced *A.M. 113682/31.M2*). Despite being four years older than the school, RAF Manston would have to wait even longer before being awarded a badge and crest.

The first section of the Ramsgate Tunnels was opened on 1 June 1939 by His Majesty the Duke of Kent, who took a tour around them accompanied by the Mayor of Ramsgate, Arthur Boomfield Courtnay Kemp. On 27 May 2014, almost seventy-five years later, the tunnels were opened again, as a tourist attraction, thanks to the efforts of Phil Spain. Ironically, the tunnels were officially opened by the Duke's son—the present-day Duke of Kent.

Grp Capt. W. V. Strugnell handed over command of HQ RAF Manston to Grp Capt. Alexander Gray in July. Grp Capt. Gray was a former soldier who had served in both the Highland Light Infantry and the Argyle and Sutherland Highlanders. He had been commissioned into the 7th Battalion of Princess Louise's Regiment (Argyle and Sutherland Highlanders) in October, but then re-mustered to the RFC in September 1916. By the end of 1917 he had been appointed as the Commanding Officer of No. 55 Squadron, but in July 1919 he suffered a serious accident when he was struck by the propeller of a D.H. 4.

After recovering from what could have been a fatal injury, Gray went on to study at Cambridge University in 1921. However, by 1923 he was active in the RAF again as the CO of No. 12 Squadron, which was stationed at Northolt and equipped with the D.H. 9. He was then posted to a staff post in Malta. This led to him being appointed to another technical post in India, before he returned to the home establishment to take command of No. 7 Squadron. He was later appointed as the deputy director of training, and then as the deputy director of armament training—which was his last job before he arrived at Manston.

The local press reported two serious air accidents in July. Although they did not directly involve Manston, both incidents involved local people and one occurred quite close to the airfield. The first involved twenty-eight-year-old Charles Frederick Almond, a senior pilot from Ipswich who had been temporarily attached to Ramsgate Airport, and his passenger, twenty-two-year-old Henry Angwin Spray, from Plymouth.

The aircraft crashed at Ipswich Airport after carrying out a return cross-country flight to Ramsgate; it circled the airport four times before colliding with the windsock mast and crashing on the airfield. A ground engineer at Ramsgate Airport, Mr James Edward Grey, gave evidence at the inquest that the aircraft was fully serviceable and fit to fly. The inquest acknowledged that Mr Almond was an extremely experienced pilot, with 2,000 hours of flying in his log book, and so recorded a verdict of accidental death.

On 22 July the *East Kent Times* reported 'three airmen were killed and two planes were smashed to smithereens' in an air crash that had happened the previous day in East Kent. The accident involved a civil aircraft, D.H. 60 Moth G-ABJZ, and Hawker Hind K5148, which was being flown by a student of the Oxford University Air Squadron. The two aircraft collided above the desolate countryside between Sandwich and Tilmanstone, and it was assumed that the Hind belonged to a unit based at RAF Manston.

The pilot of the D.H. Moth was Mr Keith Brown, the chief flying instructor at a school based on the airfield at Bekesbourne. He was also a well-known sportsman and aviator in East Kent. His passenger was Mr Allan Pragnel, a student of the school who came from Canterbury. The pilot of the Hind was Pilot Officer David Curit Lewis, who, as it was later discovered, was stationed at Lympne. According to the report in the *East Kent Times*, the Hind had struck the Moth behind its rear cockpit, tearing off a part of the Moth's tail. The tail fell to the ground, separated from the main fuselage—in which Mr Brown and Mr Pragnell were both trapped.

The collision tore out the engine and rear fuselage of the Hind. The latter part flew on for another half-a-mile, before falling to earth and narrowly missing a farmhouse. Eyewitness Mr R. J. Hambrook, of Tilmanstone, said that the RAF aircraft seemed to stagger on through the air, with Plt Off. Lewis leaping out of his aircraft when it was still some 50 feet above the ground. He was still alive when Mr Hambrook reached the scene, but he died soon afterwards. Mr Hambrook recalled hearing a terrific crash before looking up to see two aeroplanes colliding, the silver and blue D.H. Moth disintegrating in the air.

When Mr Hambrook reached the wreckage of the Moth he found the two men on board had been pinned by their legs—he believed they must have been killed instantly. Another witness, Mrs J. Luck of Vicarage Farm, said that she had just finished dinner when she heard an explosion; she rushed out to see a yellow aircraft flying towards her, narrowly missing the roof of her farmhouse, shedding parts of its body. The aircraft ended up in a haystack at the bottom of the garden, with some parts travelling on, into the cornfield beyond it, and some pieces ending up in a tree. The bodies of the three men were taken to the Eastry Institution. There is no doubt that this was the most tragic air crash for a number of years.

In August, the *East Kent Times* reported that a mystery plane had been seen flying over Richborough—approximately two miles from the airfield at Manston. The aircraft had been spotted on the morning of Saturday 16, and on the afternoon of Sunday 17. The plane had none of the usual markings, and was described as a small, two-seat monoplane with square wings, painted a dull yellow or brown. The mystery aircraft was seen flying in from the sea over Pegwell Bay and then out again in the same direction, after making two circuits over what was then known as a Kitchener Camp.

The civilian who recognised that the aircraft was German was himself a German refugee, but it remains unclear if this was the case. If the plane truly was German, the mystery remains as to how its pilot managed to fly to Britain from an airfield in Germany; it would have needed to have flown over both Belgium and France, and to have travelled for several hundred miles. Most light aircraft did not have the fuel to fly that far. Eyewitnesses claimed that something had been thrown from the plane towards the grounds of the Kitchener Camp—a search was carried out, but nothing was found, and it was suggested that the object may have simply been oil or exhaust being emitted from the engine. It is not beyond the bounds of possibility that the aircraft had been specially adapted for long-distance flights, and it is not unlikely that the Germans would have sent a reconnaissance aircraft over Southern England.

At some point in late 1939 the Luftwaffe did take an aerial photograph of RAF Manston, which clearly highlights the airfield and buildings on the domestic site. The word 'Rollfeld' is written across the grass runway, and various hangars and buildings are marked and identified using the letters A–G. The grass runway is marked with the letter 'G', but the letter 'E' also appears on the grass on the eastern side of the airfield. What is most interesting is that the letter 'E' also marks what appears to be a small network of trenches on the edge of the domestic site; it is obvious that the Germans were taking a keen interest in activities at Manston.

With the declaration of war just days away, there were further changes being made to the command of No. 3 SoTT. On 24 August Wg Cdr Benson was posted to No. 2 Group Bomber Command for mobilisation duties. He was later posted overseas, and served as a staff officer in India and at HQ Air Command in South-East Asia.

Sqn Ldr A. H. V. Hayman took over command of the unit, only to be replaced the following day by Sqn Ldr O. W. Clapp. Clapp had been the principal of the de Havilland technical school, which was originally based at Stag Lane, London, before being moved to Hatfield.

The order was given for general mobilisation on 1 September. The strength of No. 3 SoTT at this time was;

Civilian Employees	68
Officers	8
Education Officers	10
Civilian Officers	2
Airmen Posted	954
Attached	29
Total	**1,071**

An aerial reconnaissance photo of RAF Manston, taken in 1939. (*RAF Manston History Museum*)

The following day, 200 personnel who had been detached to Manston for a training course were returned to their units, and the Air Navigation School was transferred to St Athan. After nineteen years of operation, this was the end for No. 3 SoTT—it would be dispersed to other RAF stations. The ORB entry for 3 September simply states: 'War declared against Germany'.

The first unit to arrive at RAF Manston following the declaration of war was No. 3 Squadron, which came in from Croydon on 10 September. It was equipped with the Hawker Hurricane Mk.1, and was under the command of Sqn Ldr H. H. Chapman—who had only been appointed in August. He had been awarded a short-service commission in April 1928, and a permanent commission in September 1932 after serving with No. 56 Squadron. Before being appointed to command No. 3 Squadron, his previous post had been as a signals officer with No. 22 (Army Co-Operation) Group. On this occasion No. 3 Squadron only had a short stay at Manston; they returned to Croydon on 17 September. However, they would later return.

A wartime training syllabus came into effect on 4 September, and Fg Off. A. Marlon and 43 personnel (comprising No. 1 Section staff and trainees) proceeded to No. 5 SoTT at Locking. On the same day, Fg Off. B. J. Abraham, 119 personnel (comprising No. 3 Section staff and trainees), and sixty-nine MT vehicles left for No. 4 SoTT at St Athan, near Cardiff. The remaining forty-two members of No. 3 Section left for St Athan the next day, along with 5 MT vehicles.

This is thought to be the full complement of pilots from No. 3 Squadron, posing for a photograph at Manston. (*Author's collection*)

A number of pilots from No. 3 Squadron shortly after arriving at Manston, discussing tactics while standing in front of a Hurricane. The pilot in the middle of the group is thought to be Flight Lieutenant Berry. (*Author's collection*)

In October, the CO of HQ RAF Manston, Grp Capt. Gray, was posted to No. 9 Group HQ at Barton Hall, near Preston. He was replaced by Grp Capt. R. H. Hamner, who had served with No. 88 Squadron in the First World War. Hamner was mentioned in RAF Communique No. 29 for his actions on 18 October 1918; he had destroyed a Fokker biplane after being attacked by four of them. He had been posted to No. 43 Squadron in January 1932—he was mostly associated with this squadron, and was later appointed as CO.

On 23 October No. 3 SoTT was re-established at Blackpool, under the command of Grp Capt. C. B. Cooke. Workshops were established in the Corporation Garage and Tramway Department in Talbot Road, and in the Ribble Bus Company garage in Devonshire Road. Within a few weeks, the training of flight mechanics, flight riggers, and drivers was getting back to normal at the school. Trainees were initially billeted at the town hall before moving to a house in Raikes Road, while the officers were accommodated in the Regal Hotel.

The airmen posted to Blackpool from Ramsgate had effectively exchanged one seaside town for another, but the difference was that the whole of Blackpool was occupied by the RAF. The airport was occupied by two permanent units, the famous Blackpool Tower became an experimental radar mast, and there were various training units spread throughout the town.

A further two units arrived at Manston at the end of October—No. 235 and No. 253 Squadrons. However, at this point neither squadron had any aircraft, and were waiting to be equipped with appropriate equipment for their roles. No. 235 Squadron was allocated to fighter command, and was waiting to receive Fairey Battles for training purposes. No. 253 Squadron was commanded by Sqn Ldr Eric Douglas Elliot, who had been confirmed with the rank of Pilot Officer in December 1928. He later became quite a controversial character. The unit had been designated the role of shipping protection, and should have received Bristol Blenheims, but none were immediately available—so it was also equipped with the Fairey Battle.

No. 79 Squadron replaced No. 3 Squadron on 12 November, under the command of Sqn Ldr Colin Campbell McMullen; it was equipped with the Hawker Hurricane. This squadron had been formed from 'B' Flight of No. 32 Squadron in March 1937 at Biggin Hill. McMullen had been awarded a short-service commission in November 1931, and a permanent commission in November 1936. Not long afterwards, the unit was credited with destroying their first enemy aircraft—this was also the first enemy to be destroyed by a plane flying from RAF Manston.

On 21 November, three aircraft in 'Yellow Section' were ordered to patrol off the coast of the English Channel near Folkestone. However, due to engine trouble only two planes got airborne. The two pilots who successfully took off were Fg Off. James William Elias 'Jimmy' Davies, the leading Flight

Commander, and Flight Sergeant F. S. Brown. Davies was born in New Jersey, but he was of mixed Welsh and American descent. He had joined the RAF in 1936 on a short-service commission, and had been posted to No. 79 Squadron on completion of his training.

Shortly after they began their patrol they spotted a lone Dornier 17. Both No. 79 Squadron pilots took turns attacking the Dornier, which was seen entering a dive before spinning into the sea off the coast of Deal. It was confirmed that the Dornier had been destroyed. It was the first enemy aircraft to be brought down over the English Channel, and also the first by a squadron that was technically still based at Biggin Hill. Davies was later awarded the DFC for this feat.

On 4 December No. 79 Squadron was given the responsibility of providing top cover over a Royal Navy destroyer which was conveying the King to France to meet British troops. Six days later the unit again provided cover for the King while he safely returned to Dover. The unit was proud of the fact that it had prevented the Luftwaffe from attacking the destroyer, ensuring the King's safety.

Those at Manston were probably puzzled by the strange sight of a Vickers Wellington bomber which had been converted for general reconnaissance use. No. 1 General Reconnaissance Unit arrived at Manston on 12 December, and its Wellington Mk. 1s were fitted with a huge ring (48 feet in diameter) used to degauss magnetic mines. The ring was made out of lightweight Balsa wood, and contained an aluminium coil. It ran just in front of the nose of the aircraft, under the wings, outside the arc of the propellers, and halfway down the fuselage towards the tail. When an electrical charge of approximately 500 amps was passed through the coil, it detonated any magnetic mines that were in its path. Only a small number of Wellingtons were ever converted to this role—because of problems with weight, all the guns and turrets had to be removed from the bomber, and the aircraft's crew had to rely on a fighter escort for defence.

A detachment from No. 600 (City of London) Squadron arrived at Manston on 27 December, to be equipped with the Bristol Blenheim 1f—a long-range fighter version of the Blenheim 1 Light Bomber. The Blenheim 1f was woefully slow, with a maximum speed of just 278 mph, and it was therefore unable to compete with the modern generation of fighters. Following an Air Ministry decision in 1938, 200 Blenheim 1s had been fitted with a gun pack underneath the fuselage, which housed four Browning .303 guns to complement the Vickers 'K' gun. The 'K' gun was located in a semi-retractable hydraulic turret, fitted in the fuselage behind the cockpit.

No. 600 Squadron had been formed in October 1925 at Northolt as the first Auxiliary Air Force Squadron. As a day-bomber squadron, it had been equipped there with the D.H. 9A, but in 1934 it was re-equipped with the

Hawker Demon and changed its role to a fighter squadron. It had been re-equipped with the Blenheim 1f in January 1939, while stationed at Hendon, but in August 1939 it moved back to its original base at Northolt.

Most of No. 600 Squadron's Blenheims had only been recently fitted with the Airborne Interception Mk. III Rader (AI) at St Athan. Although the unit was meant to operate in a night-fighter capacity, it inevitably ended up flying daylight operations. The unit would become a regular visitor to the airfield, beginning as a detachment but soon becoming a semi-permanent unit.

A Bristol Blenheim, similar to the type operated by No. 600 Squadron. This aircraft was one of the first entered into service, and it served with No. 62 Squadron. It is seen here at Abingdon, at Empire Air Day 1937. (*Author's collection*)

13

Beyond the Call of Duty

On the first day of 1940 the strength of RAF Manston was 116 officers and 1,877 other ranks. Wing Commander Jordan was the Commanding Officer at HQ, and the Adjutant was Squadron Leader E. S. Osborn.

At the beginning of the year a large number of civil aircraft entered into service with the RAF, and were given military serial numbers. Among the aircraft at Ramsgate Airport were: D.H. 87 Hornet Moth G-ADMM, which was allocated the serial W5755; Short Scion Senior G-AECU became HK868. Lord Beaverbrook's Lockheed 12 Junior Electra, G-AEMZ (a regular visitor to Ramsgate and Manston), was allocated as R8987. These types of aircraft were mainly used for communication duties.

The year did not begin well for some units based at Manston. The first casualty was suffered by No. 79 squadron; a Miles Magister being used as the squadron hack crashed near Margate on 2 January, killing the two men on board. The incident occurred after Pilot Officer Lewis had requested to take a member of the ground crew up for a flight in the Magister. Flight Commander Fg Off. Davies gave permission, but told Lewis to check with the 'B' Flight Commander. If he agreed, Lewis was to enter this in the 'B' Flight authorisation book.

After receiving approval for the flight, Plt Off. Lewis took off in Magister P2508 with his passenger, LAC Needham. Fg Officer Davies watched the aircraft climb to approximately 2,000 feet, before being shocked to see it roll over and carry out an inverted glide towards the ground. The aircraft finally recovered at around 200 feet. When Lewis landed, Fg Off. Davies said that if Lewis ever did anything like that again he would ground him. Davies also told him that he would report the matter to the CO in the meantime.

A short while later Lewis was seen taxiing out in the Magister again, this time with AC Smith as his passenger. Those who witnessed his departure said that he was going excessively fast. The aircraft successfully took off, but soon afterwards two Manston airmen (at home, on leave) observed the plane carrying out aerobatics and flying inverted. One of the airmen then witnessed the aircraft going into a dive from which it failed to recover—it crashed into the ground, in a near vertical position. Both airmen were killed instantly.

Plt Off. Thomas Spencer Lewis (4041) was buried in his home town of Llanishaw, near Cardiff. Aircraftman 2nd Class Sidney Herbert Smith (620008) was buried in Westcott's Holy Trinity churchyard. During the subsequent inquiry, Fg Off. Davies testified that Lewis was normally a careful pilot—but that he could be a little temperamental. The court found that the cause of the accident was Lewis flying too low when he began to carry out the aerobatic manoeuvers. However, it could not rule out that the rear-seat passenger had unwittingly obstructed the controls.

After arriving in Manston in December, the Wellingtons of No. 1 GRU had been equipped with directional wireless installations (DWI)—but that was just a ruse, diverting attention from their true purpose. They carried electrical equipment that had been built by a company called Maudslay, powered by a Ford V8 petrol engine. Under the control of No. 16 Group, the Wellington's magnetic ring was first used successfully on 8 January, when one of the aircraft flew over and detonated a magnetic mine laid by the Germans. There was further success on the 15th, but on this occasion the Wellington flew beneath the specified safety height of 35 feet—it suffered some damage, but managed to land safely.

The weather at the beginning of 1940 was very bad. The ORB for No. 600 Squadron gives the most accurate account of conditions at that time; for example, on 15 January, the ORB stated that a heavy snowstorm had reduced visibility on the airfield to less than 70 yards. By the evening, the aircraft was completely buried in snow and unfit for flying, with further snowfall over the night.

The beginning of 1940 was relatively quiet compared to later in the year, with the exception of the odd skirmish when pilots encountered a lone Heinkel or Dornier. Six Hurricanes of No. 79 Squadron were sent to patrol Hawkinge on 13 January; the patrol included Fg Off. Mitchell, Plt Offs Morrice, Parker Hulse, and Clift, and Sergeant Spencer.

The bad weather also brought ill health, and in the middle of January a number of No. 79 Squadron pilots became sick with influenza while others suffered from the measles and tonsillitis. Flight Lieutenants C. L. C. Roberts and R. S. J. Edwards were also grounded because of the flu; three pilot officers suffering from German measles were also grounded.

Despite the continuing wintry conditions, the taxing abilities of a number of Blenheims were tested on the morning of 17 January. There were also subsequent examinations on their undercarriages, airscrews, and air intakes. On the 19th No. 600 Squadron were allocated the use of the firing ranges at Sutton Bridge—however, the weather prevented any of the aircraft from taking off. The next day was a similar story; the temperature dropped down to -6°C and there were strong winds that caused the snow to drift. The day was spent checking and re-aligning the gun sights, which in most cases were found to be only slightly out of alignment.

The cold weather continued to affect operations at Manston throughout late January and early February; after being closed for several days at the end of January, the airfield began operating again on 2 February. No. 253 Squadron had started to receive their Hurricanes, and on the 14th a batch of nine was delivered to Manston. In the middle of February the unit began to dispose of its Fairey Battles, flying them out to No. 22 Maintenance Unit at Silloth. Only five remained at Manston.

On 12 February the severe cold closed the station again, preventing No. 253 Squadron from flying its aircraft out to Northolt—the squadron was due to move there on the 14th. It was several days before the weather was good enough for the aircraft to fly, but by the end of the month the squadron had been established at Northolt with sixteen Hurricanes, five Battles, two Magisters, and one Miles Master. The squadron was comprised of nineteen officers (eighteen of which were pilots) and 176 other ranks, including five sergeant pilots. Twelve pilots were detached to Uxbridge for a short course on fighter command tactics and radio telephony.

On Friday 16 February No. 79 Squadron suffered another fatality. Twenty-six-year-old Fg Off. James J. Tarlington (40763), flying a Hurricane L1699, failed to return from a convoy patrol over the North Sea; he had been patrolling a train ferry off Reculver, where there had been no reports of enemy action. The aircraft entered service with No. 32 Squadron at Biggin Hill in November 1938, and had been transferred to No. 79 Squadron in March 1939.

His aircraft was observed crashing into the sea by an officer in the coastguard, who claimed that the Hurricane had ditched just 1 mile off the coast of Reculver. A search was carried out by the Margate lifeboat *Lord Southborough* and the Minesweeper L67 that was serving with Nor Command. Despite an extensive operation, Tarlington's body was never found; it was suspected that either an engine or oxygen failure was to blame for the crash.

Newly-promoted Sqn Ldr James Wells arrived at Manston on 18 February, taking over command of No. 600 Squadron from Sqn Ldr G. L. S. Dawson (Viscount Carlow). Sqn Ldr Wells' father also had a title—Wells was the son of Sir Sydney Richard Wells and Mary Dorothy of Felmersham, Bedfordshire. The unit would soon become one of the only permanent units to be based at Manston.

On 2 March a high-flying aircraft was seen over Dover, making a vapour trail at approximately 25,000 feet. It was suspected that this was an enemy reconnaissance machine, and Fg Off. Davies led three Hurricanes to try and intercept it. However, the unidentified aircraft flew out to sea, too high and fast for the Hurricanes to get anywhere near it.

No. 32 Squadron came to Manston from Gravesend on 8 March, relieving No. 79 Squadron which returned to Biggin Hill. However, much of the month was dominated by the arrival of Polish airmen from Eastchurch. One hundred and twenty arrived at Manston on 11 March, ninety-three on the 15th, and sixty-five on the 20th. All of these airmen had to be accommodated and issued rations; the majority would be sent to Squires Gate at Blackpool Airport, where a special unit had been set up to teach them English and RAF procedures. Although individual airmen had already been serving with a small number of units, there was still some opposition to allowing the Polish or Czechoslovakians to form their own squadrons.

There was another serious incident on 11 March. A Blenheim of No. 600 Squadron, L6682, had carried out an army co-operation searchlight exercise and was on approach to the flare path when it struck some trees. The pilot, Fg Off. Anthony Hamilton Tollemache, survived. Despite being very badly burned, he tried to rescue one of the passengers—2nd Lieutenant Philip Rowland Sperling, who was serving with the Welsh Guards. LAC Smith, one of the other members of the crew, was thrown clear, but Sperling was trapped in the wreckage; despite Tollemache's brave efforts, he could not be saved.

2nd Lt Sperling was buried in his home town of Kingsclere, Hampshire, on 16 March; Fg Off. Tollemache was later awarded the Empire Gallantry Medal for his brave efforts to rescue him. The citation read:

> With complete disregard of the intense conflagration or the explosion of small arms ammunition, he endeavoured to break through the forward hatch and effect a rescue. He persisted in this gallant attempt until driven off with his clothes ablaze. His efforts, though in vain, resulted in burns that nearly cost him his life. Had he not attempted the rescue it is considered that he would have escaped almost unscathed.

Tollemache's EGM was later exchanged for a George Medal. The burns he suffered were so severe that he became one of Archie McIndoe's 'guinea pigs' for his new and innovative treatments. He later returned to the service, and had another lucky escape during the Normandy landings, where he acted as a liaison officer—the tank he was travelling in was hit by enemy fire, and the man standing next to him had his head blown off.

Tollemache was killed in a car crash in Paris in 1977; he was sixty-three years old. He was survived by his wife, Celia, who remained living at their home in Ely. Eleven years later, in 1988, the house was burgled; the George Medal, along with four others, was stolen. Celia was in hospital at the time of the robbery, and the burglars took advantage of the fact that the house was empty. Ten years later the medal was mysteriously found on a tourist beach on Queensland's sunshine coast, Australia, many thousands of miles from where it had been stolen. It was handed over to the British Consulate in Brisbane before being sent back to Britain and handed over Tollemache's two sons—

who loaned the medal to the RAF museum.

On the night of 14–15 April, twelve Handley page Hampdens of Nos 44, 50, and 83 Squadrons were diverted to land in Manston. They had been engaged in the first mine-laying operations of the war—named the 'gardening sorties'—and had laid mines in the sea lanes between German ports, Denmark, and Norway. Twenty-eight aircraft were involved in the operations, and two of them were lost after enemy action. The first of these was Hampden L4152 of No. 83 Squadron (based at RAF Scampton), which was captained by Fg Off. Kenneth Richard Hugh Sylvester (39907). It was last heard of sending a distress call at 4 a.m., trying to home in on Manston; it never arrived, and was presumed lost at sea. The other aircraft was Hampden L4113 from No. 61 Squadron, based at Hemswell—it vanished without a trace.

At the end of April it was decided that No. 32 and No. 79 Squadrons would take turns as the defending fighter units at Manston; each squadron would be detached to Manston for a week at time, after which they would hand over to the other. The ORB on 10 May noted that the intensification of the war situation meant that security had to be tightened; detachments of the London Irish Regiment and the Royal Artillery arrived at Manston with anti-aircraft guns.

The 10 May was a bleak day for Europe—Germany began its invasion of Belgium and Holland, with thousands of parachute troops being dropped at strategic places. The Germans had begun their bombardment of the Dutch airfield at Waalhaven, Rotterdam, at 4 a.m., and an hour later 500 troops (*Fallschirmjagers*) parachuted onto the airfield. The Dutch held out for a while, and the airfield was still not completely under German control by the time that the airborne troops began landing on the battlefield. However, by 6.30 a.m. all resistance had ceased; there was little the Dutch could do in the form of immediate resistance, and so London was contacted for help in attacking German-held airfields.

No. 600 Squadron was ordered to attack the airfield and shoot anything on the ground, especially German Ju 52s—troop-carrying transports. Six Blenheims took part in the raid, with crews led by thirty-one-year-old CO Sqn Ldr Wells. He flew in Blenheim L6616 (BQ-R), accompanied by crew navigator Sgt John Davis and air gunner Corporal Basil Arthur Kidd (who was thirty years old). The six 'B' Flight aircraft took off from Manston at 10.30 a.m. on what some must have known was a very dangerous (if not suicidal) mission.

Sqn Ldr Wells made the decision to leave the navigators of the other five Blenheims behind at Manston, aware that his was the only aircraft that carried three crewmen. Sqn Ldr Wells and Sgt Davis had sole responsibility for finding their way to the target—from which only one Blenheim would return.

The other Blenheims and crews that took part in the operation were: L1335 (BQ-W), with pilot Charles R. Moore and Air Gunner Corporal Basil A. Kidd; L1401 (BQ-K), with Fg Off. Hugh C. Rowe and Plt Off. Robert H. Echlin;

L1514, with Plt Off. Norman Hayes and Cpl J. Holmes; L1515, with Plt Off. Michael H. Anderson and LAWC Herbert C. W. Hawkins; and L1517 (BQ-N), with Plt Offs Richard C. Haine and M. Kramer.

As would be expected, Sqn Ldr Wells led the attack, followed closely by Plt Off. Hayes—who later claimed that he had destroyed at least one Ju 52 by setting it on fire. It is believed that L1335, with Fg Off. Moore and Cpl Isaacs, was the first Blenheim to be shot down. They were attacked by eighteen Bf 110s of 3/ZG 1, and crashed on or near to the airfield.

The Blenheims stood little chance against such powerful opposition. They were outnumbered three to one, but they were also outclassed in both speed and armament. Sqn Ldr Wells' Blenheim crashed in the village of Pernis; although he and Kidd were killed, he had managed to hold the aircraft steady enough for navigator Sgt Davis to bale out. Fg Off. Rowe and Plt Off. Roberts crashed in the village of Piershill; the pilot was killed, but the air gunner survived (despite being knocked unconscious). He was pulled out of the wreckage, and was taken as a prisoner of war after spending some time in hospital.

Sqn Ldr Wells was the second of three brothers to be killed in action. The other two were Lt-Cdr Christopher Hayward Wells (Wing Commander) and Major Thomas Clapper Wells. Lt Cdr Wells was thirty years old when he was killed on 8 June 1940, serving in the Royal Navy on the HMS *Glorious*. Lt Cdr Wells was the only one of the three brothers to be married—his wife was Christine Wells of Toronto, Canada.

Sqn Ldr Wells' other brother, Maj. Thomas Clapper Wells, served in the 5th Battalion of the Bedfordshire and Hertfordshire regiment. He was killed whilst serving in Singapore on Friday 13 February 1942; he was shot in the head while on observation duty. He was buried in the Kranji War Cemetery. A memorial stone, which commemorates all three brothers of the Wells family, was later dedicated and placed on the wall of Felmersham Church.

Plt Offs Haine and Kramer managed to execute a forced landing in the Netherlands, and made their way to a village that was still being held by British troops; they were joined there by Sgt Davis, the navigator from Wells' crew. The three airmen were put aboard the destroyer HMS *Hereward* (H Class 'H' 93), commanded by Lt Cdr C. W. Greening, along with the Dutch Queen Wilhelmina—who escaped on the same ship. They arrived back in England on 13 May.

The only aircraft that made it back to Manston was the L1514, flown by Plt Off. Norman Hayes—but his aircraft had been so badly damaged that it was written off. While they were flying away from the target area, the L1514 had encountered a formation of three He 111s, and air gunner Cpl Holmes had used up all the remaining ammunition to escape. Hayes was not sure how they had managed to survive the carnage, but remembered that after the main attack he had flown east for a short while, towards Germany, before heading back to Manston. Plt Off. Hayes was later awarded the DFC, and his Air Gunner, Cpl Holmes, was awarded the DFM for his part in the raid. The citation for Plt Off. Hayes' DFC read:

> This officer was the pilot of one of six aircraft which attacked Rotterdam aerodrome in May, 1940. In company with his Commanding Officer he destroyed a Ju 52 on the aerodrome by machine-gun fire. Whilst climbing, after the dive, the formation was attacked by twelve Me 110s.

Sqn Ldr de B. Clarke took over command of No. 600 Squadron, and it was soon back in action. On 13 May a crew from the unit filed a combat report with No. 11 Group, regarding an incident that had taken place on the 11th—when 'Green 1' of 'B' flight had engaged a He 111. There had been seven enemy aircraft in the skies, but 'Green 1' only engaged one of them, 20 miles north-west of Cape Gris Nez at 7,000 feet. Three bursts of eight seconds had been fired at the Heinkel, and a small amount of white smoke had been seen coming from its engine. On returning to Manston it was discovered that the wheel and flaps of 'Green 1' could not be lowered, but none of the crew were injured in the subsequent forced landing.

No. 604 Squadron arrived at Manston from Northolt on 16 May, with No. 600 Squadron travelling in the opposite direction. No. 604 'County of Middlesex' Squadron was under the command of Sqn Ldr M. F. Anderson, and similarly to No. 600 Squadron it was equipped with the Blenheim 1f. It would remain at Manston for just over a month.

The Wellingtons of No. 1 GRU departed from Manston on 18 May, bound for the Middle East. They initially operated out of Ismaïlia, in Egypt, with one of the support aircraft being P2522. They arrived at Ismaïlia on the 22nd, and were engaged in work on the Suez Canal, but they later transferred to other areas and operated out of LG 05.

On 23 May Sqn Ldr F. Laurie White, the CO of No. 74 Squadron, had to make a forced landing at Calais-Marc after combat with a Hs 126, a single-engine aircraft used by the Germans for army co-operation and reconnaissance. What followed was something that would not have been out of place in a *Boy's Own* story.

Although Calais was not to surrender until 26 May, German forces were quite close and White was in imminent danger of being stranded. Grp Capt. Bouchier, at Hornchurch, devised a daring plan to rescue him which involved flying a Miles Magister from Manston, escorted by two Spitfires. The Magister was flown by the No. 54 Squadron CO Sqn Ldr James Anthony Leathart, known on the squadron as 'the prof'.

The two Spitfires were flown by Plt Offs Al Deere and John Allen of No. 54

Squadron, and they were successful in making sure that Leathart's Magister landed safely in Calais. They picked up Sqn Ldr White, but after leaving Calais they came under attack from a dozen or more Bf 109s. Plt Off. Deere was credited with destroying two Bf 109s in the subsequent dogfight. All three aircraft landed safely at Manston.

The following day there was an attempt to recover and repair Sqn Ldr White's abandoned Spitfire from Calais-Marc. A Blenheim of No. 600 Squadron was loaded with a radiator, Glycol, and two fitters to repair the Spitfire—but by the time they carried out the work, the Germans had arrived, and both men became prisoners of war. As a point of interest, the Miles Magister that was used to rescue Sqn Ldr White survived until 1944, when it was struck off charge.

No. 12 Servicing Flight was posted at Manston from Hemlow on 24 May, but, more importantly, high-speed launches also arrived at Ramsgate Harbour to carry our air–sea rescue duties. The first to arrive was launch No. HSL101 from Newhaven on 27 May, with No. HSL100 arriving on 6 June from Calshot. The boats were part of No. 24 Air Sea Rescue Unit, and their crews were billeted in The Oaks Hotel, opposite Ramsgate Harbour—where a blue plaque commemorates their service to the town.

Twenty-two of the launches had been built for the RAF by the British Power Boat Company, and had entered service in 1937. They were numbered 100–121, their hulls were made out of mahogany, they were 64 feet long, and they had a beam of 14 feet. They were powered by 500-hp Napier Sea Lion engines,

RAF High-Speed Launch Number 127 battles its way through rough seas near Ramsgate. (*John Williams*)

Another view of the RAF High-Speed Launch. The RAF ensign is partially visible on the mast on the stern. (*John Williams*)

A photograph of an RAF High-Speed Launch from 24 Air Sea Rescue Unit, believed to be HSL 100, in Ramsgate Harbour. (*John Williams*)

A group of airmen from 24 Air Sea Rescue Unit relaxing for a photo. (*John Williams*)

with a top speed of 39 knots—fast, compared to other types of vessels.

Although many of those left stranded on the beach at Dunkirk claimed they had been abandoned by the RAF, there is a lot of evidence to prove the contrary. A number of squadrons based at Manston and elsewhere were involved in the evacuation, and many of the pilots found themselves on the wrong side of the English Channel during Operation Dynamo (26 May–3 June). No. 54 Squadron's Plt Off. Deere was shot down on 28 May, and had to return courtesy of the navy—as did Plt Off. Smart of No. 65 Squadron and Sgt S. L. Butterfield of No. 213 Squadron, who returned on the paddle steamer *Royal Eagle*.

A large number of small boats took part in the operation, but one which must be mentioned is the M.Y. *Sundowner*, which had been requisitioned by the admiralty on 31 May. The boat was owned by Cdr Charles Lightoller, who had been the most senior officer to survive the sinking of the *Titanic* on 15 April 1912. Lightoller was adamant that, should his boat be requisitioned, he, his son (an eighteen-year-old sea scout), and his crew should be the ones to take it to Dunkirk.

The *Sundowner* left Ramsgate Harbour at 10 a.m. on 1 June, and approximately halfway across the Channel they came across the 25-foot motor-cruiser the *Westerly*—which had broken down, and was on fire. Cdr Lightoller took on the two-man crew and the three men they had just rescued from the beaches—all of whom had to temporarily return to the horror they had so recently escaped. At Dunkirk, Lightoller found that that the wall of the jetty was too high to allow troops to board directly, and so men were transferred across from the Royal Navy Destroyer HMS *Worcester*.

Cdr Lightoller had heard that his older son, 2Lt R. L. Lightoller (later Lieutenant-Colonel), had been evacuated to the beach forty-eight hours earlier—and it had been in his mind that he might meet his son and rescue him. However, the crew of the *Westerly* told the Commander that most of the men from his son's unit had already been taken off, so he abandoned the idea of searching for him. It is claimed that that the *Sundowner* returned to Ramsgate Harbour with 150 men crammed into her cabin and many others out on the deck, but there are some who think this figure was exaggerated. There have been many arguments over the years over whether it was Ramsgate or Margate that received the most servicemen, but it is now generally accepted that it was Margate.

Cdr Lightoller had three sons; he had already lost one of them in service to the RAF. Fg Off. Herbert Brian Lightoller had been killed in action on 4 September 1939; he had been the pilot of Blenheim IV N6189, which had taken off from RAF Wattisham, along with three other Blenheims from No. 107 Squadron, to attack Wilhelmshaven. All four aircraft were shot down—Lightoller's Blenheim crashed near the target area, killing all three of the crew. He was twenty-one years old. Of the twelve airmen who made up the other four crews on the Wilhelmshaven raid, only two survived; Sgt G. F. Booth and 1st Class AC L. J. Slattery became the first airmen from Bomber Command to become PoWs. Sadly, Frederick Roger Lightoller, who had accompanied his father in the *Sundowner* in June 1940, was killed while in the service of the Royal Navy in February 1945.

Cdr Charles Lightoller died on 8 December 1952, at the age of seventy-eight. The *Sundowner* is still berthed in Ramsgate Harbour, and acts as a living memorial to those who were evacuated from the beaches at Dunkirk. Along with other small boats that took part in the evacuation, the *Sundowner* makes regular trips to Dunkirk in order to keep the memories and spirit of Operation Dynamo alive.

There was another change of command at RAF Manston on 12 June, when Wg Cdr Richard Bowen Jordan took over from Wg Cdr Hanmer. The thirty-year-old Wing Commander, a former pupil at Marlborough School, had joined the service in 1921, and he had been amongst the first students to study at the RAF College at Cranwell. It had become the first military college in the world when it opened in February 1920, and Jordan had excelled in sport there, playing cricket and rugby. He was awarded a permanent commission in 1922, and later served on Nos 2 and 28 Squadrons, before being appointed to a staff post at Ralpur, India. His last post before arriving at Manston had been as CO of No. 83 Squadron.

However, similarly to his predecessor, Jordan's time at Manston was very short indeed; he arrived on 12 June and handed over his office on the 20th. He later recalled that he was only there for the period of Dunkirk, and his responsibility had been re-fuelling, re-arming, and feeding the pilots and ground crews from eleven group squadrons. He handed over command to Sqn Ldr E. S. Osborn, who had been promoted to Squadron Leader in August 1939.

A crew from No. 604 Squadron claimed its first victory on the night of 18 June, when one of its Blenheims shot down a Heinkel 115 Floatplane. This type of aircraft was used by the Luftwaffe as one of its principle maritime attack aircrafts, as a torpedo-bomber, and for general reconnaissance. The aircraft carried a crew of three, and had entered Service with the Luftwaffe in September 1933. The airman who felled the He 115 was Flt Lt Alistair Stewart Hunter (90222), who had joined the service in 1937 and was called to full-time duty in August 1939. On this night Hunter was accompanied by observer Sgt Gordon Sinclair Thomas. Hunter and Thomas reported that they were certain the He 115 had crashed off the French coast, but the Luftwaffe did not list it among the nineteen aircraft they recorded as losing that day. As it was a seaplane, there is always the possibility that it force-landed on the sea and survived.

The night of 18 June saw the first heavy bombing raid on Britain by the Luftwaffe, and Canterbury was under a yellow warning on two occasions. A few day later, on 20 June, No. 604 Squadron moved back to Northolt from Manston, where it was relieved by No. 600 Squadron. Twenty-four-year-old Flt Lt Hunter did not survive the war—he was killed on 6 February 1941, while still in the service of No. 604 Squadron.

Another He 111 was shot down in the early hours of 19 June, and this time there could be no dispute about its fate. It crash-landed on the beach near Margate, and was clearly visible, sitting on the beach—as a result, the Heinkel was visited by hundreds of local people. The enemy aircraft (radio call-sign '5J+FP'), had taken off from Melville and was shot down by Fg Off. George Eric Ball of No. 19 Squadron. He was born and raised in Tankerton, just up the coast from Thanet, and had studied at St Lawrence College in Ramsgate—almost a local lad.

The Heinkel was flown by Plt Lt Hans-Jurgen Bachau. It had been caught in the searchlights near Colchester, and engaged by Fg. Off Ball. One of the crew, Feldwebel Reitzig, attempted to bale out of the stricken aircraft, but when he jumped out his parachute got caught in the tail. Bachaus was probably aware of what happened, and tried to get back across the Channel to France—but his aircraft was too badly damaged. However, he made an excellent forced landing on the beach at Sackett's Gap, near Palm Bay, and a photo taken at the time suggested that the Heinkel was more or less intact. Bachaus and the two other crew, Unteroffiezers Theodore Kuhn and Fritz Boeck, were taken as prisoners of war; Reitzig was buried in Margate Cemetery.

Fg Off. Ball had joined No. 19 Squadron at Duxford in February 1938. On 26 May he had been credited with destroying a Bf 109, but he had been wounded during this combat. Of the five pilots engaged in the same operation, two of his colleagues from No. 19 Squadron had been killed, one wounded, and another taken as a PoW. Ball was posted to No. 242 Squadron a few days after shooting down the Heinkel, and he went on to survive the war; by 1946 he had been promoted to the rank of Squadron Leader. Sadly, he was killed when he lost control of a Gloster Meteor of No. 222 Squadron while carrying out aerobatics.

At the end of June an air-experimental station was established at Borstal Hill, Whitstable, and it was placed under the control of RAF Manston. This Type 31 Radar Station was twinned with another at Dunkirk, near Canterbury, and was part of the Chain Home Low system which covered the southern and eastern coast. The Luftwaffe began avoiding the south coast after the fall of France—especially when attacking the north of England. In order to avoid detection they flew up the west coast, through St George's Channel, because there was no radar cover here until the end of 1940.

The first raid on the airfield took place on 3 July, when a number of high-explosive and incendiary bombs were dropped—some of which fell dangerously close to the explosives store. Manston may not have been the

Heinkel A1 + JP, which crashed at Goodman's Farm on 2 September after it had been attacked by Fg Off. Ball of No. 19 Squadron. The pilot, Feldwebel Karl Eckert, was badly wounded; the observer took over the controls and landed the aircraft. Three other members of the crew were wounded, including Gefraiter Hans Köhler, and both he and Eckert died a few days later. Eckert was buried in Margate Cemetery, Köhler in Ramsgate Cemetery.

Heinkel 5J + FP of 6/KG4, which crashed into the sea off Sackett's Gap on 9 June; it had been shot down by Fg Off. George Ball, of No. 19 Squadron. Its bombs had been jettisoned before it ditched into the sea; one of the crew, Feldwebel Alfred Reitzig, baled out, but his parachute was caught in the tail and he was killed. This photograph was taken after the aircraft had been pulled from the water.

main target, as the ORB describes the event as a raid on the local district. Sgt John Rex Burgess White (743734), of No. 74 Squadron, was killed after his Spitfire (K9928) was struck by lightning; this caused the aircraft to burst into flames and crash onto an area of land known as The Shallows, between Margate and St Peter's. Sgt White had previously served with Nos 151 and 72 Squadrons, and had joined No. 74 Squadron on 10 May; he was buried in Highgate Cemetery, London.

Two days later, No. 1 'M' Balloon Unit arrived at Manston. This was not a balloon unit in the traditional sense—it was equipped with totally different balloons, used to form a barrage. The balloons that No. 1 BU used were approximately 10 feet in diameter, and filled with 520 cubic metres of hydrogen. No. 1 BU would dispatch these balloons into the air, where they would travel as far as Germany on the air currents; here, their payload of propaganda leaflets would be released.

The balloon unit had been set up under the control of Bomber Command, soon after Germany had invaded Poland. The unit was commanded by a flight lieutenant with experience of meteorology. Its aim was to launch up to twelve balloons an hour, and up to five hundred per week. The unit was initially deployed in France (with the first contingent of the Advanced Striking Air Force), and had completed its first operation from Foug airfield, on the outskirts of Nancy, on the night of 30 September 1939.

Plans to evacuate the unit from France began on 16 May, and its personnel managed to escape with its main equipment via Nantes and Cherbourg, on their way back to Britain. The 'M' Balloon Unit was transferred to Balloon Command and posted to Manston to overcome the security problems; operations from Manston began on the night of 16–17 July.

A clockwork mechanism had been originally used to release the propaganda leaflets, but a burning fuse was later fitted which destroyed the balloon while safely releasing the leaflets. A system had also been fitted to allow for the leakage of hydrogen from the balloon during the flight to the target area—sandbags or small packages of leaflets would be jettisoned, allowing the balloon to regain altitude. The areas targeted from Kent were Hamburg, Breslau, and Saxony, but rogue balloons are known to have reached as far as Italy and Spain.

The CO of No. 65 Squadron, thirty-three-year-old Sqn Ldr Desmond Cook (26009), was killed when his Spitfire (K9907) was shot down off the coast of Dover at 3.30 p.m. on 8 July. Sqn Ldr Cook came from Cyprus, and he was the son of Harry L. and Dorothy Cooke, of Kyrenia. Three Bf 109s were shot down over the course of the afternoon—including one piloted by Lt Albert Stiberny, who baled out of his aircraft near Sandwich.

A Heinkel He 59 ambulance aircraft was forced down onto Goodwin Sands on Tuesday 9 July. Although such aircraft displayed the Red Cross, it was known that they often acted as spotters, reporting shipping movements to German aircraft. The He 59 had first flown in 1931, and was a biplane powered by two BMW 660-hp engines, fitted with two large floats. No. 54 Squadron was climbing out from Manston at 8 p.m., on the way to intercept other enemy aircraft, when they spotted the He 59 at 1,000 feet—escorted by twelve Bf 109s.

The aircraft may have been on its way to rescue a downed German pilot from the sea; however, there was a precedent for enemy aircraft abusing the Red Cross—this included He 59 D-ASAM, which had flown over Sunderland on 1 July. The No. 54 Squadron pilots were taking no chances, as Plt Off. Al Deere (a New Zealander) ordered Plt Off. John Allen to attack the Heinkel, while the other section went after the fighters.

The He 59 bore the civil registration letters 'D-ASUE'; it was painted all white, with red crosses on its nose and a swastika on its tail. It was forced down onto the sands by a section led by Plt Off. Allen, and it landed in one piece—with its four-man crew quickly evacuating the aircraft and taking to a rubber dinghy. The aircraft was later taken in tow by the Walmer lifeboat, and beached on the sands at Ramsgate.

In the action that followed, Al Deere very nearly met his end; his Spitfire, N3183, collided with a Bf 109, but his luck held out and he was able to make a forced landing in a field near Manston. It was not the first time that Deere had escaped from the jaws of death—he had been shot down over Nieuport, in France, on 28 May. It would also not be the last. Two other members of No. 54 Squadron were not as lucky; Plt Offs Garton and Evershed were killed, with the former being shot down near Manston and the latter near Dover. Plt Off. Jack Wallace Garton (70887) was buried in Margate Cemetery, while the body of Plt Off. Sydney John Anthony Evershed (80810) was never recovered—he is commemorated at the memorial at Runnymede.

On Wednesday 10 July, the official starting date of the Battle of Britain, No. 74 Squadron was attacked while on convoy duty from Manston. It was using Manston as a forward base, along with No. 56 Squadron. It is claimed that No. 74 Squadron seriously damaged a number of Dorniers, which were trying to bomb the convoy it was screening. By this time, Manston was known to most of the pilots of Fighter Command by the codename 'Charlie Three'.

One of the first RAF aircraft to be shot down during the Battle of Britain was Hurricane P3554 of No. 56 Squadron, flown by Plt Off. E. J. Gracie, on 10 July. Fortunately the pilot was spotted in the water, 10 miles north of Herne Bay, by the crew of a Lysander, V9545—he was rescued by a fishing boat. The Lysander almost certainly belonged to No. 4 (Army Co-operation) Squadron, which had been evacuated from Dunkirk and was probably based at Hawkinge.

The action was becoming more intense, and RAF Manston's defences were reinforced as a result. The army positioned 3.7-inch guns at Ozengell Grange, on Haine Road, to the east of the airfield, and at Chalkhole Farm (better

Leutnant Schauff's Last Flight. A painting depicting the last moments of Lt Josef Schauff, of 8/JG26, when he was shot down over Margate. (*Geoff Nutkins*)

known today as Little Cliffsend Farm). In 2014, two large bunkers which housed former naval guns still exist on the cliffs close to the farm. Most of the other defences comprised of light .303 machine guns, mainly manned by air gunners and other members of No. 600 Squadron.

There were a number of high-profile visitors in July, the first being by His Royal Highness the Duke of Kent (who held the rank of Group Captain) on the 18th. He was to become a regular visitor to Manston, and would support the people of Thanet during their darkest moments. Two days later, the Secretary of State for Air, Sir Archibald Sinclair, visited Manston, and on the last day of the month the Inspector General of the RAF, Air Chief Marshal Sir Edward Ludlow-Hewitt, inspected the station.

Plt Off. John Laurence Allen was killed during a convoy patrol on 24 July, just over two weeks after the incident involving the He 59. The engine of his Spitfire, R6812, failed, and the aircraft stalled and crashed into an electric sub-station on Omer Avenue, Cliftonville, at 12.30 p.m. Allen's Spitfire was the first RAF aircraft brought down on the Isle of Thanet during the period of the Battle of Britain. He had been credited with destroying seven enemy aircraft, one of which was No. 54 Squadron's first claim of the war—over Dunkirk, on 21 May. He had escaped death on a number of occasions, including when he had crashed in Scotland on 18 January 1938 and had become trapped in his cockpit for twenty hours.

Unteroffizier Fritz Buchner, who was killed when his aircraft crashed at St Nicholas-at-Wade. His remains were not recovered until 1975. (*Nigel Douglas*)

During the same fight in which Allen was killed, German Lt Schauff of 8/JG 26 baled out of his Bf 109 over Margate, after being attacked by Plt Off. Gray of No. 54 Squadron. Unfortunately, his parachute failed to open; Schauff plummeted to the ground, his body landing on a local playing field. His aircraft crashed in Byron Avenue at 1.05 a.m., one of six enemy aircraft shot down in the air battle over Margate. Another German plane had to force land at Northdown, but its pilot escaped with minor injuries. Lt Josef Schauff was twenty-one years old, he was from Lippo-Bergheim, and had been credited with destroying one British aircraft—a Hurricane, shot down on 8 June.

Plt Off. Allen was buried in Margate Cemetery on 29 July, the same day as Plt Off. Archibald Finnie (79158), another pilot from No. 54 Squadron. Finnie had been shot down near Dover at 6.10 p.m. on July 25, while on a convoy patrol. He had been attacked by a Bf 109, and his Spitfire, R6816, crashed near Kingsdown. No. 54 Squadron's ORB refers to the 25th as 'Black Thursday'—it had lost another pilot, twenty-two-year-old Flt Lt Basil Hugh Way (33402), in addition to two Spitfires. Plt Off. Turley-George was shot down near Dover, but fortunately he was uninjured and his Spitfire, P9387, was later returned to service.

Plt Off. Finnie had only joined No. 54 Squadron on 8 July, and was the same age as Plt Off. Allen—just twenty-four years old. Airmen from Manston acted as pallbearers, and Sqn Ldr Osborne presided over the funeral; as usual, the coffins of the two airmen were covered with the Union Jack. The site where they were buried already contained forty-six graves, mainly those of British and French soldiers and sailors who had been killed during the evacuation of Dunkirk. There were many floral tributes to the two airmen, and one of them read: 'Good flying and happy landings from the mother of another pilot. Rest on the wings of God.'

There was a third funeral at Margate Cemetery, on the 29th, for Lt Josef Schauff. He was afforded the respect shown to all enemy aircrew; his coffin was draped with the Swastika flag of Germany, and amongst the floral tributes was the message: 'You had no other choice. Perhaps you will be able to understand one day. God bless you and may you rest in peace.' This probably served as a reminder that the war was being fought against the Nazis, and not against the German people.

It is not known for certain who shot Allen down, but there were rumours that he had been the victim of the German ace Adolf Galland, of JG 26, who claimed a Spitfire 30 km off Margate. However, this seems unlikely, because Galland claimed that he saw his victim crash into the sea—and Allen crashed on land.

Allen had been born in Kenya on 3 July 1916. He was awarded a short-service commission in June 1937, and the twenty-four-year-old officer had been mentioned in *The London Gazette* for receiving the DFC on 11 June.

He was not forgotten in death; on Saturday 24 July 2010 there was a service of commemoration and thanksgiving for his life at Canterbury Christ Church University, on the Broadstairs Campus. The university's chaplain, Reverend Dr Jeremy Law, took the service. Allen already had a building named after him on campus, and his name also appears on the Battle of Britain monument in London—opened by Prince Charles and the Duchess of Cornwall in September 2005.

A number of dummy Hurricane and Defiant aircrafts arrived at Manston during that summer, but the exact date of their arrival is unknown. They were amongst a batch of fifty which had originally been intended for use on dummy airfields, in daylight (known as 'K' sites), but had been diverted for use on real airfields. The first dummy rubber aircraft to be used on an operation airfield had been at Drem, Scotland, where dummy Hurricanes were left on the airfield while the real ones were hidden in a wood. In Kent, the batch of fifty Hurricanes and Defiants was spread between Manston, Rochford (Southend), and Lympne, while a batch of dummy Battles went to Eastchurch. The results were not encouraging. During a three-month period there was not a single attack on dummy aircraft at an operational airfield, and they were unpopular with the AOC Flight Command ACM Dowding.

14

Exemplary Actions

Many servicemen and civilians died in incidents in and around RAF Manston during the war. The incident that most touched the hearts of the local people was probably the one which involved Flying Officer Dennis Neve Grice (70266) of No. 600 Squadron, who was killed on the morning of 8 August 1940. His Blenheim, L8865 BQ-A, was shot down over Ramsgate by a Messerschmitt Bf 109 with a distinctive yellow underbelly, flown by Oberleutnant Gerhard Schopfel of JG. 26.

Grice and his crew were Gerhard Schopfel's fifth victims; he would go on to survive the war, being credited with destroying forty-six aircraft, but he would be eventually held as prisoner by the Russians. He had originally served in the police, but had transferred to the Luftwaffe in 1936 to begin his flying training. He served with a number of different units, being given command of IX/JG 26 on 26 September 1939. His first victim was a Hurricane of No. 615 Squadron, N2331, on 19 May 1939, flown by Fg Off. R. D. Pexton. Pexton had baled out after being engaged and damaged in combat by a number of Me 109s over the north of Cambrai—but he was claimed by Schopfel. Pexton was wounded, but he survived.

In the opinion of a substantial number of eyewitnesses, Fg Off. Grice made the conscious decision to avoid crashing to the town, and struggled with the controls to avoid built-up areas. Whether this was actually what happened or not, his Blenheim was seen to crash into the sea outside the harbour at 11.55 a.m., just 400 yards outside the low-shore line. It exploded on impact, killing the three airmen on board. It was suggested in the local press that Grice might have been able to bale out of the aircraft and at least save himself—but, given the circumstances, this is highly unlikely.

Those who witnessed the last moments of Grice's Blenheim, before it plunged into the sea, were deeply affected. Sheila Cunningham and her family found the incident particularly poignant because her twenty-one-year-old brother Denis had only recently joined the RAF, training to be a pilot. Seeing the Blenheim in flames, passing low over Ramsgate and crashing, made Shelia think about what could happen to her brother. The following April her worst fears were realised. Sgt Denis Cunningham was killed while serving with No. 256 Squadron at Blackpool when the engine of his Boulton and Paul Defiant failed on take-off. Sgt Cunningham was buried at Ramsgate Cemetery.

Fg Off. Grice, the son of Neve J. and Ethel Grice and husband of Margaret Grice, came from Ealing, in London. He had joined the Reserve of Royal Air Force Officers in 1931, which meant that he had spent four years on a short-service commission, training as a pilot. He had been appointed to the rank of Pilot Officer in March of that year, and in September 1932 he was promoted to the rank of Flying Officer. This was announced in *The London Gazette* on 28 July 1939, with the note, 'Flying Officer Dennis Neve Grice relinquishes his commission on appointment to a commission in the Royal Air Force Volunteer Reserve. 7th June 1939.' Grice was twenty-eight-years-old, and had joined No. 600 Squadron at Northolt on 9 July, becoming one of the pilots detached to Manston between 20 June and 24 May the following year.

Sgt Francis John Keast (801399) was the air gunner on board the aircraft—one of the two other members of the crew. He was thirty-one years old, the son of Arthur and Ann Keast, and came from Swalecliffe, near Whitstable, just a short distance from RAF Manston. He was buried in Whitstable Cemetery. The third member of the crew was nineteen-year-old Aircraftman 1st Class John Benjamin William Warren (628894). He was the son of Jeffrey and Maud Ethel, and came from Chelmsford, in Essex. Warren had joined the RAF in November 1938, and had taken a radar course soon afterwards; on that fatal day he had been acting as the radar operator and observer. Warren's body was not immediately recovered—it must have washed ashore in France, because he is buried in Calais South Cemetery. He is also commemorated at his family grave in Writtle Road Cemetery, just a short distance away from where he and his family lived.

Fg Off. Grice's actions were recognised by the authorities; on Wednesday 7 December his wife was presented with a solid silver hand-carved cake basket by the Mayor of Ramsgate and his wife. The engraved inscription read: 'Presented to Mrs Margaret Grice by the Mayor, Corporation, and citizens of Ramsgate, as a tribute to the bravery of her late husband, Pilot Officer Grice. He died to save others.' The presentation was made during a private ceremony at a location in London, for personal reasons. Mrs Grice was reported to have said that the gift would be her most treasured possession, and a lasting memorial to her husband. The subsequent 7 December report in the *East Kent Times* (headlined 'Honouring a Hero') failed to mention the other two members of Grice's crew. This might have been the work of the censor, or perhaps Sgt Keast and AC1 Warren had been overlooked. However, the families of both of these airmen were recognised by Ramsgate Council, and presented with silver tea sets.

On the same day that Grice's crew were lost, No. 65 Squadron lost two pilots when their Spitfires were shot down over Manston, after they had been engaged by some Bf 109s of JG 26. Sgt David Ian Kirton and FS Norman Tyler Phillips were both killed in the incident. Twenty-one-year-old Kirton had been flying Spitfire K9911, which crashed while approaching the airfield from the east at 11.40 a.m. Phillips, flying K9905, hit some trees and crashed near Haine Road approximately five minutes later. Both pilots were from Kent; Kirton was buried in Dover, whereas Phillips was buried at Chatham.

No. 600 Squadron lost another Blenheim during a night patrol on 9 August, after the crew had been ordered to attack enemy aircraft dropping bombs on the Poet's Corner area of Margate. The Blenheim, L8679, was seen diving into the sea at 11 p.m. Reports suggested that it had been fired on by an anti-aircraft battery, and could have been a victim of friendly fire. The officer in charge of the guard on Margate Pier was alerted by cries for help from the direction of Margate's lifeboat *The Lord Southborough*; this vessel found and picked up the pilot, Fg Off. S. P. Le Rougetel. The other member of the crew, Sgt E. C. Smith, managed to swim ashore at Westgate.

Manston's ORB states that on Monday 12 August fifteen Me 110s and some Heinkels (later found to be Dorniers) flew over the airfield at a low level, dropping approximately 150 high-explosive bombs. Some hangars were damaged, and one civilian was killed in a workshop that was destroyed. In fact, Manston was attacked by twenty-one Me Bf 110s from Erprobungsgruppe 210, which was based at Denain, in the northern region of France. At this point it was operating out of the airfield as Calais-Marck. This group was what could be described as a 'test wing', and was being used to try out different tactics such as dive-bombing. The raid on Manston was the unit's second operation of the day; they had already attacked radar stations at Dover, Dunkirk, and Pevensey in the morning.

As the Bf 110s approached the English coast at 11,000 feet, they were joined by a group of Dornier 17s from KG-2. The aircraft dropped down to just a few thousand feet, in preparation for the low-level raid. The Bf 110s led the attack, with the Dorniers following up. There were no available RAF fighters to intercept them, but there were some No. 65 Squadron Spitfires on the ground, with their engines running, ready to take off. One of these failed to get airborne, and the pilot (Plt Off. Kenneth Graham Hart) was lucky to survive the shockwave from a bomb that exploded near his aircraft—causing the propeller to stop. Hart had only just landed to re-fuel and re-arm after shooting down a Bf 109 off the coast of Deal; fortunately, his aircraft was not badly damaged.

The raid lasted no more than five minutes, but by that time the airfield was smothered with a huge black cloud of dust. It was left heavily pitted, with at least 100 craters, rendering it temporarily unserviceable. The ORB states that the airfield was made functional the following day, but a number of deep craters remained on the southern ridge; these could not be dealt with because of the number of unexploded bombs that remained in the area.

The airfield was attacked again on Wednesday 14 August, by nine Messerschmitt Bf 110Ds of Erprobungsgruppe 210—which had again flown from their base at Denain to Calais-Marck airfield. They were made ready as early as 7 a.m., but had been delayed due to bad weather; they eventually took off at 11.30 a.m. The first Staffel planned to attack Ramsgate Airport—although this was a civilian airfield, Luftwaffe intelligence presumed it was a worthwhile target because RAF fighters could operate from it. The second Staffel had been ordered to attack RAF Manston on its own, but it was joined by the first Staffel—because two large barrage balloons, flying over Ramsgate Harbour, had prevented it from carrying out the planned attack on the airport.

The aircraft were heavily engaged by the RAF defences, who had set up Browning .303 machine guns on tripods; the Royal Artillery was equipped with 40-mm Bofors. Two of the enemy raiders were shot down, and the first Bf 110 (radio call-sign S9 + NK) of the second Staffel was claimed by airmen from No. 600 Squadron—who were manning the .303 machine guns set on top of the firing butts. The Bf 110 flew in low, above the hangar, with the rest of the formation. It was hit in the port wing, and was described as rolling slightly before diving straight into the ground, crashing inside the perimeter of the airfield at 12.10 p.m. The aircraft burned out; the pilot (twenty-three-year-old Lt Heinrich Brinker) and the non-commissioned air gunner (twenty-four-year-old Unteroffizier Richard Mayor) were both killed outright.

The other Messerschmitt Bf 110 that was destroyed (radio code S9 + MK) was also from the second Staffel, and was hit by fire from the Bofor guns of the Royal Artillery. After initially suffering damage from anti-aircraft fire, the Bf 110 possibly collided with Brinker's machine before splitting in two and crashing onto the airfield, at approximately the same time as the first enemy aircraft. The pilot (twenty-three-year-old Unteroffizier Hans Steding) was killed, but the air gunner (Gefreiter Ewald Schank) managed to bale out—a feat that was later described as one of the most amazing escapes ever witnessed.

Schank's parachuted opened just in time to save his life, and although he was badly injured he survived to be taken prisoner. In a state of shock, he was taken to a shelter where he saw soldiers with rifles and tin hats. He was surprised to encounter a soldier who spoke German, asking, 'When he would be shot?' He was later taken by car to hospital, where he spent ten days before being processed as a prisoner of war and sent to a camp in Canada.

The two Bf 110s were the first two enemy aircraft to be brought down on the airfield during the war, and both the airmen on No. 600 Squadron and the soldiers of the Royal Artillery were proud of their part in the action. Both enemy aircraft had taken off from the airfield at Benain at 11.30 a.m. The three German airmen who were killed were buried in Minster Cemetery, but their bodies were later recovered and buried in Cannock Chase Cemetery.

A third Bf 110 (flown by Oberleutnant Werner Weymann) from the first Staffel was damaged by ground fire at Manston, but managed to return to Calais-Marck on one engine. Another two Bf 110s had aborted the attack on Manston midway across the Channel, due to engine trouble; they safely returned to Calais. The raid on Manston on 14 August is recorded as occurring on the 15th in the ORB, but this is not surprising given the damage and chaos.

During these Luftwaffe raids on 12 and 14 August, an aircraft had appeared just before the main attack, painted completely black. Rumours circulated that it was a captured Blenheim which was being used to confuse the British defences, but it is more probable that it was a German aircraft. With its large glass nose, the Ju 88 was similar to the Blenheim—such a type may have been used by the Luftwaffe to co-ordinate the operation.

No. 266 Squadron, which had been reformed at Sutton Bridge in September 1939, arrived at Manston from Eastchurch on 15 August. This squadron lost two Spitfires in a strafing raid by another eight Bf 110s. The next day a Blenheim of No. 600 Squadron, R3838, and a Spitfire of No. 65 Squadron, R6618, were destroyed on the ground during another raid on Manston— although no casualties were claimed.

15

The Battle of Manston

On 15 August Margate's lifeboat, the *Lord Southborough*, received its first call out to rescue a German pilot who had been shot down at sea, off the coast of Margate. It is claimed that Feldwebbel Otoo Steigenberger was flying a Bf 109E when he was attacked by a Hurricane of No. 151 Squadron, at approximately 3.30 p.m. No. 151 Squadron was based at North Weald, in Essex, but may have been operating out of another forward airfield when they were ordered to patrol Deal at 20,000 feet.

The Hurricanes were attacked at 18,000 feet by a number of Bf 109s that were protecting a bomber formation. There is only a confusing picture of the ensuing air battle, and it is not known who exactly shot down Steigenberger's aircraft—but it was claimed by four pilots. Plt Off. K. B. C. Debenham claimed to have shot down a Me 109 west-south-west of Dover at 3.30 p.m., as did Plt Off. J. L. W. Ellacombe. On the other hand, Plt Offs M. Rozwadowski and R. M. Milne claimed to have shot down a Bf 109 south-west of Dover, also at 3.30 p.m.

A further two pilots and their Spitfires were lost on the same day. Spitfire N3189 crashed at Deal, killing pilot Sgt Hawley. After being scrambled from Manston at 11.54 a.m. the following day, No. 266 Squadron lost five more aircraft and three pilots—including its Commanding Officer. The aircraft were engaged by Bf 109s of JG 26 while climbing to 20,000 feet; Sqn Ldr Rodney Levatt Wikinson was shot down and killed in Spitfire R6768, near Deal, at 12.35 p.m. He was thirty years old, the son of Major Clement Arthur Wilkinson of the King's Shropshire Light Infantry, and he was buried in Margate Cemetery.

Ten minutes after Sqn Ldr Wilkinson was shot down, Plt Off. N. G. Bowen was also shot down and killed over Adisham, in Kent. There were also engagements over Canterbury, where Plt Off. Bazle baled out of P9312 at 12.45 p.m. However, twenty-two-year-old pilot Sub-Lieutenant H. L. Greenfield managed to get as far as Calais before also suffering a similar fate. The rest of No. 266 Squadron were ordered to land at Manston.

That evening, a Blenheim of No. 600 Squadron and a Spitfire of No. 65 Squadron were destroyed by a passing Bf 109. The following day a number of replacement Spitfires began to arrive for No. 266 Squadron, with Sqn Ldr D. G. M. Spencer taking over as CO. The Spitfires had to be parked close to one another because the airfield was still peppered with bomb craters. An attack by a Bf 109 on 18 August destroyed two of these Spitfires (X4061 and X4066), with six more being badly damaged.

No. 600 Squadron finally left Manston on 22 August; the airmen and officers of this squadron had served Manston well, both on the ground and in the air. However, they would not leave before the station suffered another attack by the Bf 110s of E 210, which dive-bombed and strafed the airfield. There were no serious casualties, but number of buildings were badly damaged, including two hangars on the east camp. The roof collapsed over a building that was being used as a temporary armoury, where a lot of valuable weapons and ammunition were being stored. The Margate Fire Brigade was quick on the scene, and much of the store was saved due to the brave acts of a number of firemen.

An attack on RAF Manston on Saturday 24 August destroyed most of the leaflets and equipment used by No. 1 'M' Balloon Unit—except for a single pair of scissors. It is not known whether the Luftwaffe was aware that the unit was operating from Manston or whether this was just luck, but the authorities suspected the former, and that the propaganda unit had become a prime target. The damage and concern over possible further Luftwaffe attacks meant that No. 1 'M' Balloon Unit moved down the road, to the village of Birchington. With a strength of two officers, and twenty-nine in other ranks, it was set up again in the grounds of Grenham School.

The 24th was the day that RAF Manston and Ramsgate suffered one of the heaviest bombing raids of the war. Approximately 500 bombs were dropped on the area in less than five minutes; it was a definitive day for the station. There were six heavy raids during the day, with the first commencing at 6 a.m., when approximately eighty aircraft crossed the coast near the North Foreland. There were further raids at 10 a.m., 12.30, pm., 3 p.m., 4 p.m., and 6.45 p.m.

After the first wave of enemy aircraft had bombed the Manston airfield, the devastation was so severe that the air was filled with thick smoke and chalk dust. The second attack on this target was prevented by the poor visibility caused by the smoke and debris, so the Luftwaffe dropped their bombs on Ramsgate Airport and the town instead. At least one aircraft (D.H. 87 Hornet Moth G-ADMM) was destroyed, being struck off charge a few days later.

Thirty-one people were killed and fifty-eight civilians were injured; local people called it 'The Murder Raid'. If it had not been for the Ramsgate Tunnels the death toll would have been much higher. The development of these

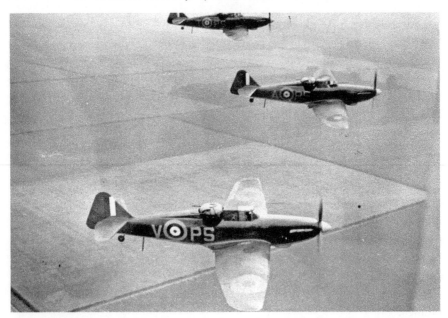

A flight of No. 264 Squadron Defiants, during a detachment to north-west England in early 1940. It is understood that the aircraft in the foreground is N1535 'A', normally flown by the unit's Commanding Officer, Squadron Leader P. A. Hunter. On 26 August 1940, he was posted as missing while flying the aircraft over the English Channel. (*Author's collection*)

tunnels was credited to Arthur Bloomfield Courtenay Kemp, known locally as the 'mad mayor', who had been elected in 1938. He worked alongside the borough's engineer Dick Brimmell to ensure that the network of tunnels (2.5 miles long and 60 feet underground) could accommodate the people of the town during such an emergency.

The RAF lost twenty fighters on the 24th, with at least seven of them in the immediate vicinity of RAF Manston. No. 32 Squadron lost four Hurricanes, and No. 610 Squadron lost three Spitfires. No. 264 Squadron was based at Hornchurch, under the command of twenty-seven-year-old Sqn Ldr Philip Agernon Hunter (32081), but it had been ordered down to Manston earlier that day. It fared particularly badly, losing four aircraft and seven airmen, including CO Sqn Ldr Hunter in N1535).

Sqn Ldr Hunter's Defiant was observed chasing a Ju 88 out to sea during the engagement; it was never seen again, and he and his air gunner (Plt Off. F. H. King) were listed as missing. The sole survivor was the pilot of L965, Plt Off. R. S. Gaskell, who survived despite his aircraft being badly damaged near Hornchurch. His air gunner, Sgt W. H. Machin, died of his wounds. However, four enemy bombers and two Bf 109s were destroyed by the crews of No. 264 Squadron's Defiants.

Oberleutnant Werner Bartels had to force-land his Bf 109E at Northdown,

Dick Hambridge (left) and Jack Foad, at the site where Herbert Bischoff's Bf 109 crashed on 24 August 1940. The photo was taken to commemorate the 60th anniversary of the incident. (*Mike Nichols*)

near Margate, at 1 p.m., after being engaged in combat with a Spitfire of No. 65 Squadron. The thirty-eight-year-old pilot was seriously wounded, and was repatriated to Germany in 1943—probably due to his age and his condition. However, Bartels was fit and healthy enough to be involved in the Messerschmitt 262 project, and it is understood he flew this type on several occasions.

The other Bf 109 E downed on 24 August was that of Felwebel Herbert Bischoff—'White 9'—which made a forced landing on the Minster Road, at Westgate, at 3.45 p.m. It was claimed by Plt Off. G. D. Gribble of No. 54 Squadron, but Luftwaffe records state that it suffered from engine failure. Bischoff was not injured, and was taken as a prisoner of war.

Many of the buildings and hangars at RAF Manston were destroyed, and those still standing were badly damaged. In addition to this, the water supply had been cut off, so there was no immediate prospect of putting out the fires. After another heavy raid, at 3.20 p.m., the decision was taken to evacuate all non-essential personnel from the airfield. It ceased to operate as a front-line airfield, and was restricted to emergency use. Of those who remained, the airmen of No. 12 Servicing Flight moved out of the main camp and were billeted in tents erected in Quex Park. Manston also renewed its relationship with Westgate, which had begun in 1916 when the landing

The main forward fuselage of the Dornier, recovered from the water upside-down. (*Copyright Mark Stanford. Courtesy of the Royal Air Force Museum*)

The manufacturer's name plate is still in position, with most details still quite clear. This Dornier was built under licence by another German aircraft-manufacturing company, Henschel, and was given 'Werke Nummer 1160'. (*Copyright Mark Stanford. Courtesy of the Royal Air Force Museum*)

One of the Dornier's two 1,000-hp BMW-Bramo 323P engines. (*Copyright Mark Stanford. Courtesy of the Royal Air Force Museum*)

A propeller from Dornier 17 Z-2 5K+GR, from KG 3, which crashed on the Goodwin Sands on 26 August 1940. (*Copyright Mark Stanford. Courtesy of the Royal Air Force Museum*)

A wing and other debris from the Dornier—in good condition, after many years in the sea. (*Copyright Mark Stanford. Courtesy of the Royal Air Force Museum*)

What looks like a propeller boss from one of the Dornier's engines. (*Copyright Mark Stanford. Courtesy of the Royal Air Force Museum*)

A flight of Hawker Auxaxes, as operated by a resident unit at Manston, No. 2 Squadron, from September 1934. (*Author's collection*)

ground at Westgate had been moved over to Manston because of safety concerns.

Street Court School and Ursuline Convent were used as accommodation for the Women's Auxiliary Air Force, while Doone House School became the Officer's mess. Senior NCO aircrew were accommodated in St Gabriel's Home, on Elm Grove Road. Away from the immediate dangers at RAF Manston, officers and airmen began to enjoy life again.

On 26 August seven of No. 264 Squadron's Defiants, under the command of Sqn Ldr G. D. Garvin, were scrambled to intercept twelve Dorniers crossing the Kent coast, near Deal, at 13,000 feet. The first three aircraft, flown by Flt Lt A. J. Banham, Plt Off. Hughes, and Sgt Thorn, were airborne at 11.45 a.m. The other four, flown by Flt Lt Colquhoun, Fg Offs Goodall and I. R. Stephenson, and Plt Off. Barwell, followed five minutes later.

Although the Dorniers were escorted by fighters, the Luftwaffe did not have it all its own way—No. 264 Squadron crews destroyed five of them, as well as a Bf 109. In in L6985, Sgt Thorn and his gunner, Sgt Barker, were credited with destroying two Dorniers and one Bf 109, which crashed at Herne Bay. Thorn and Barker were shot down at 12.10 p.m. over Chislet, but both airmen escaped with minor injuries. Plt Off. Hughes and his gunner, Sgt Gash, were also credited with two Dorniers, before landing safely back at Manston. Fg Off. Goodall was credited with a single Do 17, but his aircraft had been damaged. Flt Lt Colquhoun and his gunner, Plt Off. Robinson, were credited with damaging a Do 17 before landing at 12.35 p.m.

Seventy-three years later, Do 17Z-2—one of the KG3 Dorniers, codenamed 5K + GR—would return to Ramsgate, making headlines in the national media. It had been flown by Feldwebel Willi Effmert, who had made a wheels-up landing on the Goodwin Sands at low tide. The aircraft had turned over on its back, and only Effmert and Unteroffizier Heinrich Ritzel survived out of the four-man crew.

Two more Defiants were lost, in addition to Thorn's aircraft. One of these was L6985, flown by Sgt Banham, which crashed into the sea near Herne bay at 12.30 p.m.—killing air gunner Sgt Baker. Fg Off. Stephenson's air gunner, Sgt Maxwell, was also killed. It is widely accepted that the intervention of No. 56 Squadron in the battle prevented more losses for No. 264 Squadron. No. 56 Squadron themselves lost two aircraft in combat with Bf 109s.

It will never be known for certain who shot down the Dornier that lingered on the Goodwin Sands for many years—however, the most likely candidate is Flt Lt Colquhoun. He claimed to have damaged a Dornier, and given the evidence it seems likely that this would have been the one piloted by Effmert. No. 264 Squadron's ORB states that Flt Lt Campbell Colquhoun attacked a Do 17, 'which dived smoking from both engines but [Colquhoun] was attacked by Bf 109 and was unable to conform destruction of Dornier.' Flt Lt

Colquhoun later served with No. 66 Squadron, surviving the war and dying in 1989.

To add to the confusion, there is a mention in No. 264 Squadron's records for 26 August of the 'mythical Heinkel 113'—a German fighter, the existence of which is still debated by aviation historians. For their part in the action, Sgt Edward Rowland Thorn and LAC F. J. Barker were awarded a bar to their DFMs. These had originally been awarded for 'considerable determination and skill when engaging the enemy', and had been mentioned in an article in the *London Gazette* on 14 May. On that occasion it was claimed that they had shot down three Bf 109s, driving off a number of others.

Two days later, on Wednesday 28 August, Prime Minister Sir Winston Churchill paid a personal visit to RAF Manston. It was Churchill who coined the phrase 'Battle of Britain', when he had made an 18 June speech that declared, 'What General Weygand called the Battle of France is over. The Battle of Britain is about to begin.' Without disrespect to Churchill or anyone else, a large part of what took place could be described as the 'Battle of Manston', due to the fact it was such a crucial location in the defence of Britain.

Dressed in an RAF uniform displaying the rank of Air Commodore (an honorary rank), Churchill was said to have been appalled by the scene of destruction on the airfield. It was claimed that the carnage he witnessed was so severe that he immediately contacted the Air Ministry, ordering them to set up an organisation to repair Manston and the other airfields at once.

No. 54 Squadron was the main unit operating from Manston on that day. Among their aircraft was Spitfire R6832, which was being flown by Flt Lt Al Deere—who had previously escaped from a forced landing on 28 May and another on 9 July, near Manston, after colliding with a Bf 109. On August 28 he escaped unscathed, baling out over Detling after being shot down in error by another Spitfire. The unit lost another two aircraft on that day, including Sqn Ldr D. O. Finlay's X4053 over Ramsgate—fortunately, Finlay was only wounded.

Also on 28 August No. 264 Squadron lost three more Defiants, including two shot down over Thanet; both aircraft and crews perished. The Defiant was withdrawn from frontline service, later being adapted for a night-fighting role—for which it was a successful interim measure until the Bristol Beaufighter entered service.

Churchill had his photograph taken with members of No. 615 Squadron (based at Kenley) during his visit, standing by the wooden intelligence hut at the crossroads by the History Museum. That hut is one of a number of historical places which remain; it is a listed building, still used by the Air Training Corps to store its band equipment.

Unteroffizier Fritz Buchner was killed on 26 August, when his Bf 109 crashed near Stuart's Farm at St Nicholas-at-Wade.

His downing was credited to Fg Off. K. J. Marsden of No. 56 Squadron. The destruction of the aircraft on impact was so severe that Buchner's body could not be recovered until 1975, when he was finally buried at Cannock Chase. Buchner had been credited with a single victory, a Potez 63 which he had shot down on 19 June.

On Friday 30 August, two days after Churchill's visit, another German bomber (He 111 A1 + JP, KG 53) crash-landed near the airfield on Goodman's farm. The aircraft had taken off from Armentiers at 2 p.m., and intelligence sources discovered that its target had been the Handley Page aircraft factory at Radlett. It had been intercepted over Essex at 13,000 feet, probably by Spitfires of No. 242 Squadron, but it had also been damaged by anti-aircraft fire over Essex. Flt Lt G. E. Ball and Fg Off. N. K. Stafford may have been responsible for the Henikel's demise.

The pilot, Feldwebel Karl Eckert, was either seriously wounded or already dead by the time the observer took over the controls and made the best forced landing he could. Eckert was buried in Margate St John Cemetery, while the observer, Gefraiter Hans Köhler, was taken to Ramsgate hospital; he died on 2 September. Kohler was buried in Ramsgate's St Lawrence Cemetery. Gerfraiters Albert Klapp and Friedrick Gluck were also wounded in the crash, but they survived—alongside Feldwebel Kurt Stockl, who was the only member of the crew to escape unscathed.

The Margate lifeboat was in action again on 31 August, rescuing a German pilot of a Bf 110 which had been shot down by a Hurricane (flown by Plt Off. Gilbert, of No. 601 Squadron) at 9.10 a.m. The aircraft ditched into the sea, two miles off Foreness Point. Obergefrieter Karl Dopfer was rescued and landed at Margate, but the body of Unteroffizier Bottlob Fritz was not found.

One of the most famous pilots of the Battle of Britain crashed into the sea off Margate on 3 September. Plt Off. Richard Hilary was the son of an Australian government official, and had been educated at Shrewsbury and Trinity College Oxford. He joined the Royal Air Force Voluntary Reserve in 1939, learning to fly at Montrose, before joining No. 603 Squadron (which had been sent south to Hornchurch on 27 August). On 29 August Hilary's Spitfire, L1021, had been damaged in combat, and made a forced landing at Lympne. By the time he was shot down over Margate, Hilary had already claimed four enemy aircraft, and he had just claimed his fifth victim when his Spitfire was attacked by Hauptmann Helmut Bode of JG 26.

After already damaging his chosen target (a Bf 109), Hilary later admitted that he should have broken away—but he continued his attack, putting in another three-second burst, which not only sealed the fate of the enemy aircraft but also that of his own. Hit from behind from Bode's Bf 109, Hilary's Spitfire, X4277, burst into flames, and he had to abandon the aircraft.

Hilary had chosen to fly without wearing his gloves, and had his goggles up above his head; as a result, his unprotected eyes and hands were badly burnt in a matter of seconds. He was shot down at approximately 10.04 a.m. and was picked up by the *Lord Southborough* at 10.15 a.m., so his time in the sea was minimal.

At Margate Hospital Hilary's burnt eyes were treated with gentian violet, and his hands were treated with black tannic acid. When he was transferred to the Royal Masonic Hospital at Ravenscourt Park, in London, his treatment was changed; the gentian violet on his eyes was replaced with saline compresses, and this probably saved his sight. He was later transferred to East Grinstead Hospital, where he came under the care of Archie McIndoe— becoming another of his guinea pigs. Hilary recovered well enough to re-join active service, but he was killed while flying a Blenheim on 8 January 1943; some argued that he should never have flown again.

16

Dispelling a Myth

The claim that there was a mutiny amongst the ground crew at RAF Manston was probably the most harmful story to the reputation of those who served at the station during the Second World War. It has been alleged that the ground crew refused to service, refuel, and re-arm aircraft; during the time the author spent serving at Manston in 1968–71, there were a lot of stories told about the station by former officers—but a mutiny was never mentioned.

The term 'mutiny' arouses many different emotions, especially amongst those who have served in the forces. Although mutinies are very rare, there are records of a small number taking place, such as the one at Biggin Hill a short time after the 1918 Armistice. This had involved men of the Wireless Experimental Establishment, who found themselves living in squalid conditions in the middle of winter. The mutiny was resolved peacefully when the whole station was sent on leave by Brigadier A. C. H. McLean, returning to find most of their demands had been met.

At the end of the Second World War there was a mutiny at the RAF station at Drigh Road, in India, which also spread to other stations such as Mauripur. The reason for this mutiny was demobilisation, and the fact that airmen in India—who had been due to be shipped home, returning to their civilian occupations—were being forced to remain in the service, with no date set for their release. This dispute was not resolved peacefully, and several of the airmen who took part were later sent to prison.

In Len Deighton's 1977 book *Fighter: The Story of The Battle of Britain*, the story of the 1940 mutiny at RAF Manston was given credence. Mr Deighton claimed that terrified airmen refused to move from their air-raid shelter after an attack by the Luftwaffe on 12 August. He further claimed that CO of No. 54 Squadron, Sqn Ldr Leathart, had to stop another officer from going into the shelter and shooting the first man who refused to come out.

Sqn Ldr James John Leathart had been appointed as a Flight Commander in July 1939, and was given command of No. 54 Squadron in May 1940.

He and Fg Off. J. Allen had been involved in the rescue of Sqn Ldr White from Calais.

The claim that a mutiny had occurred at Manston laid the blame with the airmen of No. 600 Squadron, because it still had a number of personnel at the station. The No. 600 Squadron association felt very insulted by the allegation, and at one point its committee considered suing Len Deighton for libel. Sqn Ldr Bill Cardew, who had been a Sergeant Fitter based at Manston with the unit during the period in question, said he had never heard anything about a mutiny until he had read Len Deighton's book; neither had anyone else in the squadron.

The identity of the officer who started the rumours of the mutiny remained a mystery for many years. However, in 2006 Tim Vigors published *Life's Too Short to Cry*, his memoirs about serving as a pilot during the Second World War. There is a discrepancy between the account of the mutiny given by Deighton and Vigors in their respective texts; Deighton alleges that it happened on 12 August, while Vigors refers to an afternoon in September. With the passing of many years between the alleged incident and the writing of his book, Vigors might be excused for getting the date wrong; he later served in the Far East, and it is most likely that he lost his log book. However, why did Len Deighton state that it happened on, or close to, 12 August? Could it be he chose the date because he knew it was when Manston suffered one of its most devastating attacks?

According to Vigors' account, he landed at Manston shorty after it had been strafed by Messerschmitts and taxied to the nearest fuel bowser, where he could not see anyone around to service his aircraft. Vigors' account on the events of that day correlate with that of Deighton, but that still does not mean that a mutiny actually took place. Vigors continues that after landing he noticed an air-raid shelter, which he entered, finding approximately forty men inside. He claims that he immediately ordered these men outside to re-fuel and re-arm his aircraft—a sergeant stepped forward, noticing the stripes on Vigor's battledress, and apologised, but maintained that his men were staying where they were for the duration of the air raid.

Vigors then claims that he took out his father's old revolver (which he always carried), and pointed it at the sergeant's nether regions. Vigors muttered some further insults, mentioning that an old friend of his, who had been in the IRA, had told Vigors about where he should aim if he ever had to shoot an Englishman. Vigors claims that the sergeant then ran up the stairs.

There are references in Mr Vigors' story to the fact that he had a Shamrock painted on his Spitfire. Vigors also claimed that this made the sergeant realise that he had not been bluffing when he emerged from the shelter. The motif was actually an Irish tricolour, with a green shamrock painted over it, superimposed by two swords.

Vigors openly admits in his book that the decoration had been brought to the attention of Air Vice-Marshal Keith Park, the AOC of No. 11 Group. During a visit to No. 222 Squadron, AVM Park had been dismayed to see the Irish tricolour on what he described as one of the 'King's aircraft'. Park told Vigors to remove it immediately, with Vigors struggling to maintain his composure in the face of the criticism; after Park had gone, he made no attempt to remove the motif.

Strangely enough, Vigors was not the only officer to admit threatening to shoot another airman. Flight Lieutenant Peter Brothers, of No. 32 Squadron, openly admitted threatening to shoot an armourer who had failed to re-arm his aircraft. Tension was high, and both air crew and ground crew were under immense pressure. However, the truly puzzling thing is Vigors' use of the word 'Englishman'. If he did use the term in a derogatory context, we must ask the question: who was Plt Off. Vigors fighting for. He was in the British service, flying a British flag, and fighting for the cause of the British and Commonwealth people—but he was displaying the Irish flag. He was an Irishman and proud, who was prepared to openly admit that he had some vague connections with the IRA.

To be fair to Tim Vigors, he does not refer to the events that took place as a mutiny; however, because there are no similar accounts, we have to assume that what he said or wrote sparked the allegation of the so-called Manston mutiny. This takes us back to Len Deighton—it must be asked where he got his information from, and whether or not the word mutiny was merely used to arouse interest and increase the volume of sales.

It is known that there were a number of administrative and non-combatant personnel at Manston during this time, such as cooks, clerks, and store men; a number of raw recruits had also been sent from Blackpool to Manston to help repair the runways. Theoretically, during a war situation any tradesman, of any rank, could have been called to arms, issued with weapons, and ordered to fight on the front line—in reality, many would have been useless in such a situation.

The extent to which some airmen were affected by the continuous strafing and bombing is evident in the experience of Plt Off. William Walker, of No. 616 Squadron, who had been shot down over the Channel on 26 August. On that occasion he was fortunate enough to land on the Goodwin Sands, and was taken ashore to Ramsgate in an RAF launch after being rescued by a fishing boat. The following day Plt Off. Walker was transferred from Ramsgate Hospital to RAF Halton Hospital many miles away, in Buckinghamshire—but on the way they had to stop off and pick up an airman from RAF Manston. According to Walker, the airman was suffering from very severe shell shock; he attempted to light a cigarette in the ambulance, but his condition was so severe that he had not managed to do this by the time he was dropped off in London.

Airmen who genuinely suffered from shell shock can hardly be described as cowards. These men did not mutiny, but purely displayed instinctual self-preservation. For airmen to have walked out of an air-raid shelter in the middle of an attack can be described as either brave or stupid, depending on your particular viewpoint. They were in the shelters because there was nowhere else left to go, as most of the buildings and hangars had been destroyed or were on fire.

As Rocky Stockman pointed out in the third edition of *The History of RAF Manston*, there is no evidence that airmen refused to do their duty at any time. Those men in the air raid shelters had a legitimate reason for being there, they had not abandoned their post, and they were not hiding. Perhaps it is worth noting that unsubstantiated rumours do not make a case—but they do make a smear. It is the hope of the authors that this will help put an end to the story of mutiny at Manston.

17

Secrets of the Night

As mentioned in *A Detailed History of RAF Manston 1916–1930*, there had been rumours about secret tunnels and passages on and around the airfield at Manston for many years. It is now known, however, that there really is a network of secret tunnels running underneath the airfield. This knowledge is founded on good authority from a very reliable source—who wishes to remain anonymous.

Some of the tunnels were occupied by members of the Home Guard Auxiliaries, a special commando unit sometimes referred to as 'Churchill's Secret Army'. It is possible that the details of the unit were finalised on Churchill's visit to Manston on 28 August. Members of the unit were mainly drawn from local farms, who knew the land and could live off it if necessary.

The devastating attacks on Manston's airfield caused serious concerns for the authorities, who suspected it had been chosen as a key landing ground for a potential German invasion. Everyone was aware of the events at Waalhaven, in Holland, where the Germans had swamped the airfield with parachute troops, clearing the way for airborne troops to land in Ju 52 transport aircraft. When one considers the fact that the Germans were just over 20 miles across the English Channel, in Calais, it put things in perspective. With London being 73 miles away from Thanet, the enemy was three times closer to Manston than the Houses of Parliament. On a clear day, the coast of France is clearly visible from the seafront at Ramsgate; as a number of fighter pilots observed, France was laid out before them as soon as they took off.

Winston Churchill is credited with the order that British fighters should overfly Ramsgate, Margate, and Deal every morning, in order to reassure the local population that the RAF was still active. Many local residents have since recalled that their hearts were raised by the sound of the Merlin engines thundering over the town. It has always been suggested that the Germans planned to secure the Luftwaffe's air superiority over the RAF before the invasion of Britain—although this may not necessarily have been the case.

The term 'Auxiliary' was used to refer to the 'Secret Army' because they were already members of their local home guard or observer corps, and were mostly former members of the armed forces. Details of their operational bases have been released in recent years, revealing that their patrols were typically named after vegetables. However, information about their activities is still hard to access—despite the passage of seventy years. The names of the men who served as auxiliaries have been mentioned in a small number of documents and on some websites, but it is arguably unfair to name them. They took their vows of secrecy very seriously, and their views should be respected—most of the men involved would deny their participation anyway.

There was a large number of auxiliary units established on and around the south coast, but the 6th 'Thanet' Kent Home Guard Battalion was amongst the first. It is now widely known that a corn merchant from Birchington acted as the area commander, and it is claimed that he was slightly rebellious when it came to army regulations. He had a number of illustrious contacts, and many years after the war a photograph was discovered that showed him standing alongside Field Marshal General Bernard Law Montgomery.

Each patrol's Operational Base was an underground bunker, large enough to support three to six men, accessed via a balanced trap door covered with earth and weeds. The main chamber of the OB measured 12 feet by 8 feet, was made out of elephant iron, and had a floor made of either concrete or, sometimes, railway sleepers. It was self-sufficient in the sense that each OB had bunk-beds, a chemical toilet, and an emergency exit away from the main chamber. The Monkton Auxiliaries had the codename 'Gherkin', and its OB was in the chalk pit in Monkton.

The chalk pit at Monkton has had a mixed history; in 1799 it had been owned by the Whittle family, and used to keep cattle during the winter, but it had also been used to store ammunition during the First World War. A number of people who have examined the chalk pit have said that there are no signs that any covert activity took place there; however, it has been pointed out that in 1944 a huge amount of chalk and other material was extracted from the quarry, in order to build the new runway at Manston. This would have destroyed any trace of the activity.

There was another OB at Haine Brick Works, where the entrance was hidden in a wooden retaining wall, holding back an ash pit beside the work's chimney. Another group had their OB in the site of a burned-down farmhouse, and the cellar of the building appears to have been used as a chapel. It was accessed via a slab of chalk in the floor, or through another entrance down a well to the side of the house. At the bottom of the well there was a tunnel which led to the OB's main room, where arms and ammunition were kept.

A decoy site (known as a 'Q Site') had also been set up at Monckton, to deceive German pilots into thinking they were attacking RAF Manston. Each decoy site had a lighting system similar to that of a real airfield, controlled by two airmen in a shelter who were in direct contact with RAF Manston. Enemy aircraft were drawn to the Q Site during night attacks during a black-out, attracted by the lights. An explanatory note in Air 2, issued in March 1940, states how the Q site operated:

> The Operations Staff at the parent station will ring up the night dummy. Here there will be two men provided each night by the parent station taking watch and watch (alternate watches). One will probably be asleep. The man on watch wakes his companion and starts the generator. When the generator has been started up, one man goes to the control panel and switches on the correct 'T' the obstruction lights and the head lamp. The two men take it in turn to manipulate the head lamp until an aircraft is heard approaching near enough to pick up the landing 'T'. They will then switch it out and stand on watch. If the aircraft is a friend and signals by a Very Light that he wants to land, i.e. mistakes the 'Q' lighting for a real aerodrome the lights are switched off. If it is an enemy, who starts to attack the obstruction lights only are switched off (and) the 'T' flare path is left because on stations and satellites 'T' flare paths can not be extinguished in a sudden attack without great risk to personnel. The two men than take cover in their dugout and report.

There was another Q Site at Ash Level, near Sandwich, close to where a radar station was later established. The Royal Navy Dover Command also had several decoy sites, including one on the Sandwich Flats. Apart from the Q Sites, it is known that aircraft were widely dispersed to other areas on or around Manston, including two aircraft that were kept in readiness in a barn on Cheeseman's Farm.

In 2006, *Flypast* magazine published an article by aviation author Robin Brooks, who was involved in the recovery of a Pickett-Hamilton Gun Fort from the airfield at Manston. Work began to dig the gun fort out of the ground on 18 May, and it took nine days to recover its perfectly-preserved remains; it had been in the ground for sixty-five years. The inner concrete section of the fort could be raised or lowered in to the ground as required, by the use of a hydraulic jack which had been based on the standard SkyHi garage car lift. The circular fort was 9 feet in diameter, and the concrete was between 9 and 10 inches thick.

Winston Churchill had been greatly impressed by the Pickett-Hamilton Gun Fort when he saw them demonstrated during a visit to an airfield at Langley. On 12 July he wrote to General Ismay, saying that he had seen them in action and that they were an admirable means of defence against parachutists; he recommended that they be widely adopted. Each fort required 70 cwt of

A Pickett-Hamilton Fort being raised out of the ground by the 36 Engineer Regiment of the Royal Engineers, at Manston in May 2006. (*Robin Brooks*)

One of the final sections of the Pickett-Hamilton Fort being lifted out of the ground. (*Robin Brooks*)

cement, 6.5 yards of fine aggregate, and 23 cwt of steel for the frame and manholes. The cost of construction for each fort was between £230 and £250.

Although the gun forts seemed to be a practical solution to the problems of defending an airfield against airborne troops, there were a number of problems associated with their use. Access to the small, circular concrete fort was via a metal hatch-top. Conditions inside the forts for the two or three men manning them were damp, cramped, and dismal, so they would not have wanted to stay down there for long. However, if they were to be any use, their crews would have to be in place before any attack took place, and this could mean many hours spent in the gloomy and claustrophobic atmosphere.

One document states that the normal complement for each fort (which became known as the 'pop-up pillbox') was five men, and included a Garrison Commander who gave orders to the other four men to raise or lower it. It was claimed that it took four men just four seconds to raise the fort, and ten seconds to lower it and make sure it was not an obstruction. The men were equipped with no more than a Bren gun or standard .303 rifles, so it may have not taken enemy troops too long to locate and overrun each fort and destroy or trap the crew inside.

It is estimated that 300 Pickett-Hamilton Gun Forts were produced and put in place at many of the RAF's airfields. The typical number of Pickett-Hamilton Forts on each airfield was three. Airfields where they were established included Hornchurch, North weald, Wattisham, and Stradishall. It is believed that Manston also had three, but the only other one which was found was close to the grass runway; as Robin Brooks has explained, it was flooded—like many others. The fort excavated from Manston was given to the Lashenden Air Warfare Museum, which is based on a former advanced-landing ground at Headcorn, in Kent.

We will never know how effective any of the above types of military systems and operations would have been should the Germans have invaded, because that scenario fortunately never played out. The Q Sites were the only facility put into operation. Every airfield in the country had both K and Q sites—some more than one—and there is no doubt that these did confuse the Luftwaffe crews, drawing bombs away from their parent stations.

18

After the Battle

Squadron Leader Gordon Ashley Leonard Manton took over as the Commanding Officer of RAF Manston on 5 September, while Sqn Ldr Osborn was posted to Croydon. Manton was already an experienced fighter pilot, having joined the service in June 1931. He trained at No. 2 Flying Training School at Digby, from where he was posted to the prestigious No. 111 Squadron in July 1932 (then based at Hornchurch). Manton arrived at Manston at a most crucial period, when it had been so badly bombed that it was effectively out of action. He would remain in command there until March 1941.

On the same day Manton assumed command, an enemy Bf 109E force-landed in the area of Monkton Farm, and the circumstances it were slightly unusual. Most Luftwaffe pilots who flew Bf 109s were dedicated fighter pilots, but the pilot flying the aircraft which force-landed on Monkton Farm was an exception. Wilhelm Meyerweissflog was a fifty-one-year-old technical officer attached to JG 53, who had flown as an observer during the First World War—he was no fighter pilot.

Having seen the younger pilots climbing into their aircraft and taking off from Etaples airfield, he may have become slightly envious—he decided that he too fancied going off on a sortie. Meyerweissflog climbed into a spare aircraft and took off, heading in the direction of England. Somewhere over the English Channel his aircraft was attacked by Spitfires of No. 234 Squadron (based at Middle Wallop), who may have been operating out of a forward airfield. Fortunately, his aircraft was only damaged, and he was able to make a forced landing without being injured. It is claimed that when he was apprehended he openly admitted that he had no idea where he was.

His Bf 109E displayed the markings 'No. 1', but it also had a red punishment band around the nose, approximately 1 foot wide, between the spinner and the air intake. The so-called punishment band had been painted on all of JG 53's aircraft to hide the squadron's motif: the 'Pik As', or Ace of Spades. This was carried out on the personal orders of Herman Goering when he had found out that the CO of the unit—Major Hans-Jurgen von Cramon Taubadel—had a Jewish wife. In retaliation, some of the German pilots painted over the Swastikas on their aircraft; however, the one that Meyerweissflog flew still displayed the emblem on its tail and fuselage. The matter of von Cramon Taubadel's wife was soon resolved when he was moved to another unit, and pilots of JG 53 were then able to remove the red bands and display the 'Pik As' again.

The pilot credited with shooting Mayerweissflog down was twenty-three-year-old Australian Flight Lieutenant Peterson Clarence Hughes, of No. 234 Squadron. He was credited with fifteen enemy aircraft—the highest-scoring Australian pilot—but he was killed on 7 September, just a few days after the incident involving Meyerweissflog.

On 6 September another Bf 109 of JG 53 crash-landed, close to the airfield on Vincent Farm, at 6.30 p.m. The aircraft was being flown by Unteroffizier Hans-Georg Schulte when it was attacked and badly damaged near Dover, by Spitfires of Nos 41 and 222 Squadrons. It bore the marking '5+1', and closer examination revealed that it also had a red punishment band painted around its nose; the Swastika on this aircraft had been painted over in retaliation. Schulte had claimed seven victories; the first one had been on 14 May 1940, and the last one was a Spitfire, a few minutes before he was shot down. His Bf 109 was later transported to Sheffield, where it was put on display to raise money for the war effort.

The Bf 109 piloted by Unteroffizier Schulte. It was shot down near Vincent Farm on 6 September, before being put on display at an unknown location. (*John Williams*)

Ramsgate Airport was used as a satellite station and emergency landing ground during the period of the Battle of Britain, but it had been badly damaged by bombing. The airport was shut down after the battle, and wooden stakes and other obstacles were placed on the runways to prevent enemy aircraft or gliders landing on it.

The 'Manston Spy', Herman Görtz, was back in business in September 1940. He was released from prison and repatriated to Germany earlier in the year, where his offers to work for the German intelligence services had finally been accepted. He made a number of useful contacts in the IRA while in Maidstone Prison, and he was parachuted into Ireland with the aim of setting up a network of agents that would help the Nazi cause.

Görtz was given a Telefunken set for communications, and enough money to set himself up in the town of Templeogne, near Dublin. Fortunately, the Irish police were aware of Görtz's activities; he and other members of his network were arrested and detained in prison until 1947. When he was released he was told he could travel wherever he wished, but he was shadowed wherever he went by members of the Irish CID—who were convinced that Görtz had established a large and powerful Nazi organisation.

When he was eventually informed that he would be repatriated to Germany, Görtz became distraught; he was probably deeply affected by the fact that he had failed in his two attempts at espionage in Britain and Ireland. It is also likely that he was disturbed by the thoughts of what would happen to him when he returned to Germany. It was all too much, and he took his own life by swallowing a poison capsule on Friday 23 May 1947; he was buried in a cemetery in Dublin, with a Nazi flag draped over his coffin. It was a long way from the small bungalow in Birchington where Görtz had begun his spying exploits, and it was a sad end for a man who probably wanted no more than to serve his country.

The Secretary of State for Air, Sir Archibald Sinclair, visited Manston again on 21 September to assess the damage and state of morale at the station. The following day, two Westland Lysanders from No. 4 Squadron arrived at Manston to support the high-speed launches in their Air Sea Rescue duties at Ramsgate Harbour. The aircraft were powered by 890-hp Bristol Mercury air-cooled radial engines, had fixed undercarriages, and had a stalling speed of just 65 mph. The Lysander could fly slowly and low enough to see downed airmen in the sea; not only were they able to guide surface vessels to them, but they were also able to drop dinghies and supplies. The unit was based at Linton-on-Ouse, in Yorkshire, and it provided crews to maintain and fly the aircraft.

At 2.50 p.m. on 30 September, four small bombs were dropped on the corner of the Manston airfield by a Ju 88—yet they failed to explode. Not all of the German bombs were meant to go off immediately; some were either timed to explode later or were booby-trapped.

Air Chief Marshal Sir Edgar Ludlow Hewitt, the Inspector General of the RAF, paid another visit to Manston on 1 October. The ACM was quite connected with those in the ranks, and had tirelessly campaigned for all the members of the aircrew to be given a professional status—such as the aircrew category of Air Gunner, which had been established in 1939. He had been instrumental in establishing the Central Gunnery School, and also in changing policy; especially when it was realised that daylight bombing was not practical, and the use of fighter escorts or a change to night-bombing was needed.

Small-scale attacks on Manston continued throughout October, but they were nowhere near as intense as the earlier raids. For instance, on 11 October, at 2.45 p.m., just a single bomb was dropped on the station's swimming pool. The ORB subsequently noted that this made little difference anyway, as the pool had already been totally wrecked.

The main event in October occurred at 3.45 p.m. on Thursday 17, when a Bf 109 from Jagdgeschwader 53 Unit ('Yellow 1') landed on the airfield after being disabled in combat. The pilot was Staffel Captain Oberleautnant Walter Rupp, who had previously claimed two British aircraft—the first of these being a Hurricane, south of London, on 29 September. Krupp had escaped death or serious injury on at least two occasions, and had been wounded on 21 May when his aircraft had been shot down by a Curtiss of the French Air Force.

On 10 May Rupp's aircraft had been accidentally rammed by a fellow Luftwaffe pilot (flying another Bf 109), and he had to make a forced landing at Gravenmacher. The pilot who was credited with shooting Rupp down was Plt Off. Draper, of No. 74 Squadron. This was almost certainly Bryan Vincent Draper, who would go on to rise to the rank of Squadron Leader—he was killed while in the service of No. 45 Squadron, in February 1945.

An incident occurred on 21 October which seems to prove that RAF Manston was inactive—if not abandoned—at this point, with no fighter cover at all. The station ORB noted that an aircraft, identified as a Dornier 215, dropped three small bombs on the airfield and had then flown overhead for ten minutes. It was fired on by anti-aircraft guns during this time, but it remained unchallenged by any fighter aircraft. It seems fairly obvious that the aircraft was taking reconnaissance photos of Manston while flying overhead—otherwise its crew would not have stayed so long.

Although Manston was barely operational, it provided safe haven for the crew of a Wellington who were returning from an operation over Eindhoven in the early hours of 22 October. Their aircraft had taken off form Mildenhall at 6.05 p.m. on the 21st, and had been part of a force of thirty-one Wellingtons and eleven Whitleys which had attacked targets around Cologne, Hamburg, Stuttgart, and Reisholz. The crew of R3158 (No. 75 Squadron) were captained

A Junkers 88, similar to the ones which flew over Margate—using the town as a 'starting point' for the Luftwaffe's raids on London. This was one of two that crept in under the radar at Lytham, near Blackpool, on 2 July 1942. (*Ron Collier*)

by Fg Off. R. E. Elliot. It had narrowly avoided flying into barrage balloons above Ramsgate Harbour, and Elliot was fortunate that he had been able to make a forced landing at all. Despite the misty conditions limiting visibility to less than 100 yards, Elliot was able to put the aircraft down without sustaining any injuries to the six-man crew.

'M' Balloon Unit was back in action on the night of 31 October–1 November, from its new position at Grenham School in Birchington. Seventy balloons were released overnight, with their intended destination being split between Rostock and Utrecht. By the end of that year it was releasing 1,400 balloons a month, with over 3,000,000 leaflets—and it would continue to operate from Birchington until June 1942.

At 11.30 p.m. on 2 November, Ramsgate was attacked by a large number of enemy aircraft before the air raid siren had been set off. Six people were killed and twenty-three were injured when the gas works received a direct hit and exploded, while over 100 houses were destroyed.

The ORB recorded very few details of any form towards the end of the year, providing further evidence that that the station had been virtually abandoned. However, an incident on 27 November did receive a mention—another Bf 109, 'Black 12' (flown by Lt Wolfgang Teumer), made a belly-landing on the airfield. Teumer had been attacked by three Spitfires but he was uninjured, and

The electric sub-station on Omer Avenue, Cliftonville, in Margate, where Fg Off. John Allen crashed his Spitfire on 24 July 1940. (*John Williams*)

the RAF were pleased to have captured an enemy Bf 109 E virtually intact. The captured Bf 109 was used to carry out comparability tests against the Spitfire and Hurricane; it was later put into storage, but it is now on display in the Battle of Britain section of the RAF Museum at Hendon.

Another incident on 27 November got a mention in Manston's ORB, when another Bf 109, flown by Lt Wolfgang Teumer, 'Black 12', made a belly-landing on the airfield. His aircraft had been attacked by three Spitfires, but Teumer was not injured and the RAF were pleased to have captured an enemy Bf 109E virtually intact. The captured Bf 109 was used to carry out comparability tests against the Spitfire and Hurricane. The aircraft was later put into storage but is now on display in the Battle of Britain section of the RAF museum at Hendon.

By November enemy forces faced so little opposition around Manston that the Luftwaffe was using Margate as a starting point from which its crews would fly towards their targets, using a stop-watch and compass. Peter Stahl, the author of *Diving Eagle*, explained how he flew over Margate in his Ju 88 on several occasions, both outbound to the target and on his way back to base—just a few hundred meters above the rooftops. When coming inbound, they flew just above the sea to avoid detection by radar; they regularly penetrated the RAF air defences, and rarely encountered any opposition.

On 29 November His Royal Highness the Duke of Kent visited the Isle of Thanet again, dressed in RAF uniform. He first stopped at Ramsgate, where he was accompanied by Mayor A. B. C. Kemp. It is interesting that Mr Whitney Willard Straight, the man responsible for establishing Ramsgate Airport in 1937, had up until recently been the Duke's personal assistant. Mr Straight had been called up after the war had broken out, commissioned with the rank of Pilot Officer, and had joined No. 601 'County of London' Squadron; he claimed four enemy aircraft.

As might be expected, Plt Off. Straight (90680) experienced rapid promotion; in April 1940, when he sailed to Norway, he held the temporary rank of Squadron Leader. With his vast experience of creating and building airfields, Straight was sent to Norway to find frozen lakes or other sites from which aircraft could operate. He quickly discovered Lake Lesjaskog, and arranged for it to be cleared so that No. 263 Squadron could operate from it; however, the Germans attacked the area two days later, destroying most of the Gloster Gladiators. Straight was wounded in the action and evacuated from Norway, before being appointed to the Duke of Kent's staff.

The *East Kent Times* reported the Duke's visit, stating that he had arrived in Ramsgate by car; as was his usual practice, he had driven himself, accompanied by an escort of police cars. Prior to arriving in Ramsgate he inspected coastal defences and Manston aerodrome. After being met by the Mayor and other officials, he toured the most heavily-bombed areas of the town (described as the working class area). Although the Duke drove himself around, he stopped at various points and walked along the streets, stopping to talk to local residents as he went. He then drove over to Margate, where he was met by Mayor Alderman G. P. Hoare. Here he carried out a similar tour, inspecting the damage to the town. It is interesting to note that, probably due to security reasons, the photo that accompanied the article was one of the Duke and Mayor of Ramsgate from a previous visit to Thanet.

The RAF Manston ORB has very few entries towards the end of the year, perhaps due to security concerns. There was still a limited presence on the airfield, and it is possible that there was another—unofficial and confidential— record, which has either been lost or not released to the public.

The last entry in the ORB for 1940 mentioned an unidentified raider that had flown sssover No. 1 Gun Post at a height of 8,000–9,000 feet at 7.45 p.m. on 5 December. The aircraft was heading in a south-south-west direction, and although it flew directly above the gun post it was too dark for anyone to discern the type. A number of bombs were dropped, but there was no warning—the siren did not go off until a good five minutes after the raid had begun.

Thus ended 1940, a year in which RAF Manston suffered unsustainable damage. The station ended the year as it had begun, but this time it was closed due to enemy action rather than snow. RAF Manston was down but not out, and during the subsequent years it would be rebuilt, restored, and used by the

RAF as a springboard for the attacks into occupied Europe. Such operations were given names like 'Jim Crows', 'Rhubarbs', 'Circus', and 'Rodeos'. The squadrons which flew these missions caused the same kind of mayhem and destruction on enemy-held airfields, in France, that Manston had suffered during the summer of 1940. Their crews would certainly gave back what they had endured during Britain's darkest hour.

Abbreviations

2nd Lieutenant—2Lt
Acting Commanding Officer—ACO
Advanced Air Striking Air Force—AASAF
Aide-de-Camp—ADC
Air Chief Marshal—ACM
Air Commodore—Air Cdre
Air Defence Group—ADP
Air Defence of Great Britain—ADGB
Air Force Cross—AFC
Air Force Officer—AFO
Air Marshal—AM
Air Member for Personnel—AMP
Air Ministry Order—AMO
Air Officer Commanding—AOC
Air Raid Precaution—ARP
Air Raid Preparation Committee—ARPC
Air Sea Rescue Unit—ASRU
Air Vice-Marshall—AVM
Airborne Interception—AI
Aircraftman/woman—AC
Anti-Aircraft—AA
Auxiliary Air Force—AAF
Balloon Unit—BU
Captain—Capt.
Central Flying School—CFS
Chief of Air Staff—CAS
Commander—Cdr
Commander of the Order of the British Empire—CBE
Commander-in-Chief—C-in-C

Commanding Officer—CO
Companion in the Most Distinguished Order of St Michael and St George—CMG
Companion of the Most Eminent Order of the Indian Empire—CIE
Corporal—Cpl
Directional Wireless Installations—DWI
Distinguished Flying Cross—DFC
Distinguished Flying Medal—DFM
Distinguished Service Cross—DSC
Distinguished Service Medal—DSM
Distinguished Service Officer—DSO
Elemental Flying Training School—EFTS
Empire Gallantry Medal—EGM
Fellow of the Royal Aeronautical Society—FRAeS
Field Marshal—FM
Flight Lieutenant—Flt Lt
Flight Sergeant—FS
Flying Officer—Fg Off.
Flying Training School—FS
General Duties Branch—GDB
General Renaissance Unit—GRU
George Cross—GC
Group Captain—Grp Capt.
Headquarters—HQ
Home Aircraft Depot—HAD
Hundredweight—Cwt
Junkers Ju 52, a German aircraft manufactured 1932–1945—Ju 52
King's Cross—KC
Knight Commander of the Bath—KCB
Leading Aircraftman/woman—LACW
Lieutenant—Lt
Lieutenant Colonel—Lt-Col.
Lieutenant-Commander—Lt-Cdr
Major—Maj.
Mechanical Transport—MT
Member of the Most Excellent Order of the British Empire—MBE
Military Cross—MC
Naval Air Station—NAS
Non-commissioned Officer—NCO
Officer Commanding—OC
Officer of the Order of the British Empire—OBE
Operation Record Books—ORB
Operational Base—OB

Physical training—PT
Pilot Officer—Plt Off.
President of the Mess Committee—PMC
Prisoner of War—PoW
Reserve of Royal Air Force Officer—RAFO
Royal Air Force—RAF
Royal Air Force Reserve—RAFR
Royal Air Force Voluntary Reserve—RAFVR
Royal Artillery Officer—RAO
Royal Flying Corps (1914–1918)—RFC
Royal Irish Constabulary—RIC
Royal Navy Air Service—RNAS
Sergeant—Sgt
Sergeant Pilot—Sgt Plt
Squadron Leader—Sqn Ldr
Station Commander—SC
Warrant Officer—WO
Wing Commander—Wg Cdr
Women's Auxiliary Air Force—WAAF